The Successful
Professional Practice

The Successful Professional Practice

Robert P. Levoy

Author of THE $100,000 PRACTICE
AND HOW TO BUILD IT

Prentice-Hall, Inc.
Englewood Cliffs, N. J.

PRENTICE-HALL INTERNATIONAL, INC., *London*
PRENTICE-HALL OF AUSTRALIA, PTY. LTD., *Sydney*
PRENTICE-HALL OF CANADA, LTD., *Toronto*
PRENTICE-HALL OF INDIA PRIVATE LTD., *New Delhi*
PRENTICE-HALL OF JAPAN, INC., *Tokyo*

© 1970, BY

PRENTICE-HALL, INC.
ENGLEWOOD CLIFFS, N. J.

LIBRARY OF CONGRESS
CATALOG CARD NO: 74–97581

PRINTED IN THE UNITED STATES OF AMERICA
B&P—13–868307–7

About the Author

As Director of Professional Practice Consultants Inc., in New York City, Robert P. Levoy has conducted over 2,000 management seminars for professional associations, business organizations, government agencies, and professional schools of leading universities throughout the United States and Canada. In developing these programs, he has completed more than 5,000 professional practice and public opinion surveys for individual practitioners and client firms.

He holds three college degrees in business and professional fields and is the author of over 100 published articles. His book The $100,000 Practice and How to Build It is now in its sixth large printing by Prentice-Hall, Inc.

His intensive lecture schedule, requiring more than 150,000 miles of air travel every year, combined with extensive office visits to professional practices of varying size, type and location have resulted in this unique, comprehensive guide to the successful professional practice.

Dedication

To many seminar friends
—with grateful thanks—
for much Potlatch

Table of Contents

The Starting Line

We are about to embark on a journey—a most interesting one. It has to do with practice growth and success. This can have different meanings for different practitioners.

Dr. Rollo May said, "The mark of the mature man is that his living is integrated around self-chosen goals."

Here is a list of such goals, both personal and professional, as gleaned from discussions with practitioners throughout the country. Their common thread is that they are all associated with professional practice success. You will see importance for yourself in some but not in others.

Which of the following goals best define your idea of success? Which are most meaningful to you? Place checkmarks alongside those goals you are interested in achieving. Add any others that are important to you.

We will then be ready to take that journey to greater professional success—because you will have set the course.

PROFESSIONAL GOALS

Do you want to . . .

- Do the most professional good for the most people?
- Develop more referrals from patients/clients and colleagues?
- Improve your case presentation methods?
- Develop a more effective recall and maintenance program?
- Enhance your professional stature and image?
- Upgrade and improve your fee structure?
- Increase professional income?
- Improve communications and rapport with patients/clients and staff?
- Upgrade your patient/client levels of understanding and appreciation of complete professional services?
- Engender greater patient/client acceptance, cooperation and follow-through?
- Minimize patient/client "drop-outs" and "switching?"
- Get more benefits from seminars and continuing education?
- Foster better public relations for your profession?
- Apply in-office human relations more effectively?
- Improve your technical facilities and equipment?
- Make your office more attractive, more comfortable, and more effective?
- Enlarge or build your own professional building?
- Attract new types of patients/clients into your practice?
- Simplify long-term practice management plans?
- Develop more staff "espirit de corps" and enthusiasm?
- Work at a slower pace and/or fewer hours?
- Obtain valuable "feedback" on your practice and yourself?
- See your practice in new perspectives?
- Compare your present practice methods with successful practitioners in other fields?
- Add new dimensions to your practice?

Additional Goals

1. _____
2. _____
3. _____
4. _____
5. _____

PERSONAL GOALS

Do you want to . . .

- Multiply your technical abilities?
- Be more creative?

- Be warmer, more natural with people?
- Make human nature work for you?
- Have more leisure time?
- Release your personality power?
- Break away from conformity?
- Eliminate your negative tendencies?
- Develop a more positive outlook?
- Be more "people-oriented?"
- Become a better listener?
- Increase your awareness of others' feelings?
- Become more convincing and persuasive?
- Be more enthusiastic?
- Be "above-average?"
- Eliminate some of the things in life that harass, depress and frustrate you?
- Be more adventuresome, less afraid of change?
- Develop more self-confidence?
- Instill more confidence in others?
- Be more flexible and understanding of others?
- Develop and acquire a new "self-image?"
- Overcome "stage-fright" on the speaker's platform?
- Achieve more self-fulfillment from everyday practice?
- Make your practice more challenging and interesting?
- Get more fun out of life?

Additional Goals

1. _____
2. _____
3. _____
4. _____
5. _____

—The Author

1

Toward New Dimensions in Professional Practice

A new dimension in professional practice is growing in the land. It is spurring professional people in many varied fields and practice locations to add a new ingredient to their practice.

For the past fifteen years I have been visiting professional offices everywhere and observing this dimension expressed in many ways. Wherever it is expressed—and the *way* matters little—we find professional success.

Let me try to tell you what this ingredient is, by telling you first what it is not.

It is not technical competence. Skill, technique and method are as important as ever to successful practice. They are in fact its basic dimension. But, contrary to what we learned in professional school, competence per se is not the only dimension for a successful practice. The practitioner who attains twice your practice growth, twice your success, does not have twice your technical competence. Nor does he have twice your intelligence, or twice your convictions, or twice your dedication. Call it an extra-technical dimension, if you will, but he does have "something else."

Success today requires that "something else," a new dimension which is creating a broader patient-client acceptance of full professional services.

As a practitioner you will find it an exciting safari-like experience to join me in this book to try to capture this "something else," and to harness it for your practice. We will be slaying some sacred cows together along the way, but we will be discovering some fascinating paths to the attainment of your professional and personal goals.

The "something else" is simple, yet difficult to acquire. It is volatile, yet sound as concrete. It is ephemeral, yet as permanent as people.

The safari to this new dimension starts at technical competency, travels along the way of verbal and non-verbal communication, and leads to a more *people-oriented* attitude. Along the way, and at the end of the way, we will observe practitioners in various stages of applying this new dimension and in all stages of accelerated practice growth.

PROFESSIONS AND THE PEOPLE BUSINESS

The successful professional practitioner recognizes he is in the "people business." He recognizes that people are the ones

—who consent to professional service.
—who consent to him as a practitioner of their choice in that profession.
—who consent to his suggestions, advice and assistance.
—who consent to his fees—and to paying them promptly.
—who consent to making referrals to others.

And so he understands his obligation as a professional to "reach" people as a human being himself. He accepts the premise that communicating successfully is a prerequisite for the opportunity to serve.

The new dimension is a *humanized* approach to people.

Industry and business are miles ahead of the professions in humanizing their activities. It took a receptivity to change. But when changes toward humanization were made, the acceleration of business growth was sure-fire.

Airlines that once sought predominantly to turn on speed and profits, now seek energetically to turn on people. The individual's physical and psychological comfort is now a primary concern. What used to be a passenger is now a person.

Car rental firms, hotels, restaurants are leaders in the humanizing movement and are finding that "we try harder" campaigns are paying big dividends. But all who recognize they are in the people business are making this effort to understand the psychology of human consent.

Professor Harry A. Overstreet, author of *Influencing Human Behavior,* said, "First, arouse in the other person an eager want. He who can do this has the whole world with him. He who cannot walks a lonely way."

Do you believe Professor Overstreet was talking to salesmen? He was. But, he asserted, he was also talking to teachers, clergymen, politicians, professionals, businessmen and even to members of a family.

Charles H. Brower, Chairman of the Board of Batten, Barton, Durstine & Osborn, Inc., was talking strictly to salesmen when, in 1958, he told a national sales executives convention in Washington, ". . . for this, in America, is the high tide of mediocrity, the great era of the goof-off, the age of the half-done job. The land, from coast to coast, has been enjoying a stampede away from responsibility. It is populated with laundrymen who won't iron shirts, with waiters who won't serve, with carpenters who will come around some day, maybe, with executives whose minds are on the golf course. . . ."

A little on the strong side perhaps, but these remarks make one wonder if professional men who are remiss in sharing a sincere concern for the total well-being of the patient or client, who ignore "human relations," are just as guilty of a half-done job.

Today, people are hungry for the human touch. They resent the traditional authoritarianism of professionals. They are reacting to the "don't fold, mutilate or spindle" computerized age, the overcrowding and indifference found in some professional offices. They seek, instead, more of a person-to-person relationship.

United Nations Secretary General U Thant, speaking at a public information conference in May, 1968, spoke of the importance of education. Students being trained for professions, he said, must be inculcated with "humility, modesty, compassion, the philosophy of live and let live and the desire to understand the other's viewpoint." He knows well that the Ivory Tower Attitude among individuals and groups can lead to barriers to understanding between entire nations.

The trend is already evident in American medical schools. Some medical students may soon be seeing their first patient before they get their first stethoscope. They may also be rehearsing their case presentations and bedside manners on actors posing as patients. These are some of the techniques being tried at medical schools for doctors-to-be. The object is to make the future doctor better able to cope with tomorrow's patient.

Professional associations and departments of leading universities are sponsoring seminars and workshops from coast to coast, throughout Canada and overseas, to learn how to close the "communications gap" between the ever-expanding technologies of the professional world and the patients and clients they serve. Professional people are taking these new ideas and concepts for practice growth back to their offices and initiating change.

CHANGE IS THE KEY TO PRACTICE GROWTH

Changes are needed to add a new humanized dimension to a practice. They are little changes but, regrettably, because of the anatomy of any change, they require an abundance of resolve. Few people really like the new. Most are afraid of it. Dostoyevsky said that "taking a new step, uttering a new word, is what people fear most."

I hope the excitement of adding a new dimension to professional practice and of attaining new horizons of professional services, now being enjoyed by those who do, will motivate others to overcome this resistance to change.

Former Secretary of Health, Education, and Welfare, Dr. John W. Gardner, in making his first address as a visiting professor at the Massachusetts Institute of Technology, said that one of the chief tasks ahead was change, within the framework of order, toward "a renewed quality of life, with emphasis on the importance of the individual."

PEOPLE WANT TO SHARE
THEIR PRIMARY INTEREST WITH YOU

If you are in a group photograph, whose picture do you look for first? Most people spend more time thinking about themselves than any other single subject—especially people with problems seeking professional help.

The man with a toothache is more concerned about his own plight than he is about millions of people starving in Asia. This is not to say that people do not "care." Countless do. But, as Dale Carnegie put it in *How to Win Friends and Influence People,** "You can make more friends in two months by becoming interested in other people than you can in two years by trying to get other people intertsted in you."

Patients and clients who arrive at professional offices often seem relaxed and at ease. The truth is they are tormented by worry and concern over their problems. Many are actually suffering from hypertension and acute anxiety.

Despite the natural and common sense capacity of people to grasp human relations, the science of human relations is still a relatively new one. The social psychologists have been mainly interested in large group relations. The science of interpersonal relations is left largely to the Dale Carnegies and the Norman Vincent Peales.

Successful professional practitioners have found the key to effective human relations. It is either a key they themselves have fashioned, or it is a key they have acquired from others.

Their key can be your key.

THE DOOR TO SUCCESS HAS A MASTER KEY

Professionals who have "a way with people" are not necessarily born with that blessing. They may be quite cold in reality, but they have learned how to communicate warmth.

Communication is the master key—verbal and non-verbal.

This communication takes place in many ways. And it fails in many ways.

When we talk, we don't always communicate.

When we explain, we don't always get through.

When we advise, we don't always get "heard."

Other ways in which we can either communicate or fail to communicate are:

---

* Dale Carnegie, *How to Win Friends and Influence People* (Simon & Schuster, N.Y., 1936).

In appearance.   In correspondence.
In voice inflection.   In service.
In gestures.   In mannerisms.
In office environment.   In actions.

Every one of the above methods of communication can be altered to tell a new "humanized" story. From the handshake to the case presentation, we either have the key or we don't.

WHAT THE HUMANIZED PRACTICE REALLY SAYS

A city hospital association recently launched a campaign in all member hospitals with the slogan, "Patient Care Is Our Career." Attendants, nurses, and other hospital personnel wore buttons on their uniforms bearing this message.

These buttons were *two-way* communicators:

A) They reminded the *wearer* that "people" are the most important part of the hospital, the raison d'etre for the hospital itself, that "staff" were there for *people's* convenience—not the other way around. The buttons prompted and motivated the wearer to pop into the patients' rooms with a cheery "hello," to fluff a pillow, to brighten spirits.

B) The buttons told *patients* that someone really did care in the typical busy city hospitals, notwithstanding outward appearances.

Sometimes the day just isn't long enough. We get overworked, understaffed, and pulled in three directions at once. Sometimes we forget about *people*.

In a recent magazine article, Donald Cordes, Administrator of Iowa Methodist Hospital in Des Moines, Iowa, said, "We are getting so technically competent that we are in danger of losing the tender loving care that people want above all. We try, for example, to call patients by name rather than 'that gallbladder in Room 202.' We have added to our staff a patient-relations girl to spend time with patient and family before surgery, to give a report to the family as the surgeon operates, and to go with him when he tells the results to the family."

Now, that's *caring*.

And "I care" is what the humanized practice is all about. Demonstrate "I care" to patients and clients and you'll find that you can do more for them, in terms of total service. They, in turn, will do more for you in terms of referrals and practice-growth.

The gesture of a cup of coffee, at the right psychological moment, to a person waiting well beyond his appointment or during an extended consultation can improve receptivity and communication.

An extra minute of the practitioner's time to explain a procedure, answer a question, or just listen can be the minute that is most appreciated during an office visit.

A telephone call, timed to allay a patient's or client's fears or anxieties, offers the kind of reassurance that "locks" people into a practice, cements a relationship and demonstrates the "I care" attitude of the practitioner.

It matters not, the nature of the profession. "I care" spells the difference.

ONE MAJOR STUMBLING BLOCK TO PRACTICE GROWTH

Some practitioners don't care. And they show it.

Other practitioners do care, but they don't show it.

The net result is the same: Patients and clients are left out in the cold and loneliness of their problems.

What prevents practitioners from showing that they care?

Get ready to slay the first sacred cow with me. It is called the Ivory Tower Attitude. It is an inhibitor to practice-growth. It is the vestige of a bygone era that remains do deter and obstruct. It cries for "change."

The Ivory Tower Attitude arose in the Middle Ages when a stratified society placed the professional in a class by himself. Today, the lofty purposes and idealistic goals of professions are shared by many other pursuits.

There is no foundation for a professional man to feel any of the following ingredients of the Ivory Tower Attitude:

Aloof and apart from those whom he serves.

Unconcerned with human relations.

Indifferent to the need for patient education and client motivation.

Challenged or insulted by people's questions, objections and procrastination.

Unappreciative of the opportunity to serve.

Resistant to change in status quo.

Entitled to practice success by virtue of professional training and license.

A hospital receptionist received a phone call inquiring about the condition of a Mrs. Jones in Room 688. She called the hospital floor, got the report, and repeated it to the caller. The caller thanked her so profusely, the receptionist was prompted to ask, "May I know who's calling?" The caller replied, "This is Mrs. Jones in Room 688 whose doctor never tells her anything."

Mrs. Jones' physician has the Ivory Tower Attitude. So does every practitioner who feels above doing things that show he cares. This means that most professionals have this Ivory Tower Attitude—some to extremes, some barely perceptible.

To whatever extent this attitude exists, it hinders the attainment of professional goals.

Take the most all-inclusive, idealistic goal: to do the most professional good for the most people. This goal is attained far more quickly and successfully by practitioners who have humanized their practice than by those who retain that ivory tower.

A person with problems has a tendency to throw up a barrier of protective insulation. Characterized by wariness and avoidance, it is a psychic syndrome of our time. In its normal form it protects against emotional rebuffs and permits an emotional life that is relatively free from pain. At a time of trouble, this insulation is reinforced and made double-hard to penetrate.

Yet, it must be penetrated by the practitioner who is asked for assistance. If it is not, the patient or client will be just as insulated from help as he or she is protected from hurt.

Mrs. Jones, or Mr. Smith, cannot be "reached" from the Ivory Tower.

HOW PRACTICE GROWTH OCCURS

Practice growth is a multi-factored, fluid and dynamic process. To suggest that it can be reduced to a simple "instant-success" recipe would be presumptuous. It most certainly would be an oversimplification. If such a "formula" did exist, it would of necessity be too rigid and confining. It would leave no room for self-expression and individuality. It would be in conflict with the very nature of professional practice.

The discussion of practice growth that follows is an outgrowth of our continuing surveys and seminar discussions. It is on *two* levels, both of which allow a wide latitude for personal interpretation and application.

The first is based on *new perspectives*. It will be a consideration of professional services, policies, procedures, and environment from the *patient's and client's point of view*. It will be a discussion of *their* feelings, reactions and interpretations.

Being in the "people business," these perspectives are important as guidelines for practice development. Some will be more applicable than others. Some may be surprising, perhaps disturbing. Hopefully, they will offer new insights which will serve as ground-breaking for the seeds of practice growth.

The second level is a consideration of *possible alternatives* to your present practice policies. It will be a discusion of how other professionals in varied fields handle the problems of their day-to-day practices, how they have overcome the obstacles to practice-growth and achieved professional success.

There are hundreds of ideas on the pages ahead. They are offered as *alternatives* to what you may now be doing. When all is said and done, you may feel that your present methods are best—for your personality, your practice, and your patients or clients. These alternatives then will have served to reinforce your thinking and your procedures.

On the other hand, the "new perspectives" may prompt you to take a second look at your present attitudes and methods, in which case the alternatives will be more meaningful.

First . . .

Some Semantic Shortcuts

To speed things up as we move through the practice-building concepts ahead, it would help to use some convenient abbreviations:

P/C = *Patient or Client*. The health-oriented professions speak of patients, while most of the others speak of clients. P/C refers to both. Years ago these initials were popularly known to stand for "privileged character." Let's say they still do.

ITA =   *Ivory Tower Attitude.* These initials will appear frequently and they stand for the strongest single deterrent to practice growth and the attainment of professional and personal goals.

ICA =   *I Care Attitude.* These initials represent the reverse of ITA, and its antidote. It is the essence of the new professional dimension and a humanized practice.

Potlatch = Funk and Wagnalls defines this as a gift used by American Indians. To me, it means the little niceties which evidence ICA and say "I care." Potlach can be physical or psychological—above all, it is personal.

THE ONE FACTOR THAT SPELLS REFERRALS

Every professional practice needs referrals, if only to compensate for the normal P/C attrition due to death, transfer to other areas and the inevitable "switching" that occurs in every practice.

Practitioners seeking to improve their practice need referrals even more. It matters little whether that improvement is aimed in a quality or quantity direction, referrals will be needed above the attrition rate.

When I ask seminar groups what kind of P/C makes referrals, they invariably reply, "A satisfied one." Life would be a lot easier if this were true, but it is just not so!

A *dissatisfied* P/C is certainly not long for your practice. A *satisfied* P/C, on the other hand, is likely to stay with you, but he is not likely to influence other P/Cs to join him. By definition, he's received only what he has paid for; namely, a competent, well-performed service *which he fully expected in the first place.* Having provided that, you have fulfilled your part of the bargain. The P/C fulfills his part by paying your fee. Economically and psychologically, you are "even." You owe him nothing. He owes you nothing—including, I might add, a referral.

Referrals come at a step higher, when the P/C receives *more* than he expected, *more* than he has paid for, *more* than any practitioner ever did for him under comparable circumstances.

It is these "extras," above and beyond the call of duty, that produce an *enthusiastic* P/C who talks about you, whether asked or not. It is the picture of a "missionary" for your practice.

In dealing with people, the difference between the *adequacy of satisfaction* and the *bonus of enthusiasm* requires only a little extra effort and time. But these little extra efforts are the key to referrals and ultimately determine the growth rate of everyone in business and professional practice.

Prove it to yourself. Think of a restaurant you recently tried for the first time. Was the service, the decor, the food itself just "ordinary?" Was it just "another meal?" Or, were there those "extras" that made it a memorable dinner? Perhaps the proof of the pudding, literally, was—Did you recommend it to others?

Remember the thespian masks? The big frown and the big smile? I have reproduced these attitudes below, but a third has been added between them. They illustrate well the dissatisfied, satisfied, and enthusiastic P/C.

DISSATISFIED   **SATISFIED**   **ENTHUSIASTIC***

The new humanized dimension creates enthusiastic P/Cs.

Is it belittling or demeaning to a profession to add a "human touch" here or there? The answer in this day and age is *no*. On the contrary, it is elevating to a profession.

If your practice goals include the development of more referrals, ask yourself these questions:

—Am I providing more than P/C's expect?
—Am I providing more than they are paying for?
—Am I providing more than other practitioners?
—If so, do my P/Cs *know* it?

THE FALLACY OF THE BETTER MOUSETRAP

True or False: Build a better mouse trap and the world will beat a path to your door.

With all due respect to Ralph Waldo Emerson, who reputedly made that oft-quoted statement almost 100 years ago, it is *false*. It may have been true when he said it, but in the 20th Century, the burden is on the inventor to beat a path to the consumer. People will not flock to somebody for something they don't know about.

This year 600,000 new cancer cases will be diagnosed. About 200,000 persons will be saved because they sought help. (The figure could be 300,000. But, according to the American Cancer Society, it won't be. Some 100,000 will be succumbing to ignorance, apathy, fear and fatalism.)

These statistics, and many like them referring to other professional services, indicate the need for a new perspective; namely, that people cannot evaluate, measure, or relate to an area of knowledge about which they are uninformed.

It's one explanation of:

—why people with serious problems refuse to do anything about them.
—why so many men neglect to write a will and cause their families untold difficulties in probate.

---

* For a bit of fun, I have had the "smile of enthusiasm" made up on bright yellow lapel buttons. Their use will be explained in later chapters.

—why the public neglects proper dental care notwithstanding 700 million unfilled cavities and 300 million beyond filling that need immediate extraction, according to current statistics.

Of the estimated ten million hearing-impaired persons in the United States, only two million are actually hearing-aid users. According to authorities in the field, there are undoubtedly several million more individuals who could benefit from amplification, who could perform more adequately in social and vocational situations if they wore hearing aids.

Statistics in countless other professions tell the same story. It seems people just won't beat a path to any door, even if it means better health.

Better *communication* can, however, get them interested.

HOW PEOPLE MAKE VALUE JUDGMENTS

People tend to judge the unknown and unseen by the known and seen. Illogical, but almost instinctive, is the tendency to "judge a book by its cover."

To P/Cs with whom we have talked, judgments of practitioners are all too often made, *not* on the facts as they *are*, but on the facts as they *appear* to be. And what a difference this can be!

In this regard, people react to a practitioner's recommendations by his "manner" and "attitude" as well as his "words." *Both* are important.

Everyone reacts to:

Empathy,	Understanding
Consideration,	Concern,
Love,	Appreciation.

The sum of these components is a "humanized communication." It represents the necessary connecting link between "diagnosing" and "doing," between "knowledge" and the "application of it." Its presence enables a P/C to relate to and identify with a practitioner and, ultimately, his recommendations and suggestions. Its absence explains why much of professional advice is misunderstood, misinterpreted or ignored.

In a recent study by Dr. Eli Glogow, associate professor of public administration at the University of Southern California, the follow-up appointments of clinic patients who received the standard test-interpretations and return-appointment date were compared with those who received the same, but with varying amounts of additional health information presented in a warm, personal way by someone who showed a sincere interest in each patient.

The results showed that the amount of additional health information was less important than the *manner* in which it was presented, with warmth and personal interest being the controlling factors. In an article entitled "Broken Appointment with the Doctor—What's the Reason?", published in the *Los Angeles Times* (November 11, 1968), Medical Editor Harry Nelson reported on a recent study conducted by Dr. Eli Glogow, Associate Professor of Public Administration at the University of Southern

California. In summarizing the results of the study, Nelson pointed out, ". . . a facility must provide interest, attention and tender loving care if it wants people to follow medical advice. Education comes once these things are provided."

He was, in effect, describing the humanized practice.

HOW A HUMANIZED PRACTICE BRINGS SUCCESS

After attending a seminar in Detroit, a local practitioner wrote me:

"I remodeled my office from top to bottom. I introduced procedures which I had always put off because of being 'too busy' or not 'having enough help.'
After each patient, I make myself think about what else I can do for him. It's re-markable how many things I can come up with.
Of course, I'm busier, but frankly I was already busy.
The difference is that I am so happy at the end of each day."

Happy is a big word. It is rarely used to characterize a professional practice. Yet it is perhaps the simplest word to describe what happens when a practitioner makes the little changes that add the humanized dimension to his practice.

This happiness comes from nine main sources:

—a more enlightened, appreciative and motivated patient or client.
—the gratification that a fuller professional service is being rendered.
—the practice growth that comes from patient/client referrals.
—the greater prestige that accrues from patient/client appreciation.
—the increase in leisure time that is a natural by-product of this type of practice growth.
—the enhanced self-image that prestige and patient/client appreciation bring.
—the richer and more meaningful relationships with patients and clients.
—the fuller family life that a humanized practice makes possible.
—the stimulation to further professional study and growth.

Do these alternatives to a status quo attitude sound stimulating? If they do, the change has already begun.

A Six-Day Program
to Revitalize Your Practice

The story is told of an ancient civilization which was about to be overrun by barbarian invaders. The wise men and the "scientists" of the day were worried lest their "secret wisdom" fall into the hands of the enemy and be used for evil purposes. How could they protect their secrets and at the same time insure their survival for future generations who could rediscover them? Finally, one of the elders came up with a perfect solution. They would not try to hide their secrets at all. Instead, they would publish them everywhere, write them on every wall. Everyone would talk about them and they would become axioms to which everyone was constantly exposed. That way they would become so well known, so obvious, so commonplace, that no one would pay any attention to them or bother to use them.

Today, "human relations" is a much used term and everybody knows the value of "good human relations." Yet, apparently very few people appreciate the real value or the power locked up in the right kind of human relations.

To adjust your life to reflect a greater awareness of human relations is not a matter of merely using this tool or that technique. There must be an underlying truth.

Sociologists tell us that men must learn to develop effective relationships that transcend mere decency and extend to genuine involvement in the well-being of others. And professional men are learning today that they must lead the way.

Dr. Carl R. Rogers, a Resident Fellow at the Center for Studies of the Person in LaJolla, California, told a symposium in San Francisco, "We seem to be aiming for a new reality in relationships, a new openness in communications, a love for one another which grows not out of a romantic blindness but out of the profound respect which is nearly always engendered by reality in relationships."

Efforts to bridge the person-to-person gap in the professions are resulting in impressive studies toward professional success. Certainly we all recognize that the gap needs to be bridged.

That is why:

—A hospital in Ohio hands a survey form to a discharged patient as she leaves. It asks for comments on the service and treatment and for improvement suggestions.

—An attorney in upstate New York comes out from behind his desk and pulls up a chair alongside of the client as he makes his recommendations regarding a will.

—A dentist in Southern California hands a youngster a card as he leaves the treatment room. It says, "This citation for bravery in my office entitles ——————————————————— to one ice cream cone at Stewart's Ice cream Shoppe." The youngster's name is filled in.

—An accountant in western Canada spots an item in a professional journal that applies to a client's business. He clips it, adds a personal note in the margin and sends it along.

Four apparently unrelated incidents, yet all have a common philosophy. It is to say to the P/C, "I care for you as a person, not just as a paying P/C."

The ways that a professional can express his sincerity and warmth are infinite. Examples of how others express theirs can inspire, but each practitioner must express himself in his own way.

And express he must, if the professional is to win his P/C's trust and confidence, prerequisites to practice success.

FUEL FOR CREATIVE FIRES

If we accept the truth of the old bromide that there is "nothing new under the sun," then a good definition of creativity is this: the ability to put *old* ideas together into a *new* arrangement or setting so that they suddenly produce *new* results.

At our seminars for professional groups, I have a supply of little items that I give to those who answer questions, share an idea, or contribute in some way to the proceedings. It might be a "$100,000 candy bar," a happy-button (pictured in Chapter 1), a perfume miniature, or a sample of some of the Potlatch ideas mentioned in later chapters.

It's such a little thing, but I enjoy this "give and take" with an audience. The feedback of ideas has been excellent and the result is that the programs are more lively, spontaneous, and informative.

Some of these ideas will be applicable to your practice; others won't be. Yet it is valuable for you to know what I do. And it is valuable for you to know what other practitioners are doing—others who are just as serious about their subject and service as you and I are—to evidence an awareness of "human relations."

The value lies in how it broadens your understanding, stimulates your creativity, and sparks your own inimitable expression.

As you can see, I have quite a task facing me. I have to talk with established practitioners in a diversity of professions. I must convince them that there is something they are doing that could be done better. (And, believe me, better men than I have struck out by that one.) I must develop new perspectives and suggest improvements, indirectly and by inference.

As if this is not formidable enough a task, I must do it so well that these practitioners are moved by enthusiasm to overcome the resistance we all have to change.

I'll make a deal with you. You follow a six-day program, starting today, that involves just one action on your behalf and very little expense. You will witness an immediate change for the better in your life and in your professional practice after following the following six-day program. Is one small change a day asking too much for such a reward? No? Then, it's a deal!

The First Day—Humanize Your Practice Through Non-Verbal Communication

Non-verbal communication can be even more potent than verbal. You have heard that silence was deadly and you have seen a shrug that portrayed feelings quite vividly.

A handshake, for example, can speak books. It can be strong and affirmative or it can be weak and negative. Done properly and at the right time, it is a friend-maker. More than that, it's an ice-breaker and says "I want to know you." Yet, some professional people have a reticence about shaking hands. They're too busy, or too worried about germs—or too indifferent. But our surveys show that people like to shake hands with their professional practitioners. Just as you like to shake hands with someone *you* respect and admire, your P/Cs welcome a handshake from you, whom *they* respect and admire.

Politicians know it, and after a busy campaign they usually have blistered hands. They know that this form of communication is what people want and that a good handshaking campaign creates a lot of friends and votes.

But a practitioner will benefit too, on the *receiving* end of a handshake as well as the giving. A handshake is often a giveaway as to how the P/C feels at the moment. For example, a wet, limp hand tells you this P/C may be frightened or concerned. It is a warning signal that you had better "break the ice" before you start on "official business." The P/C who is emotionally tensed-up and on-edge won't even be listening to you or receptive to your advice. This mental block will make communications difficult. At this point, you will want to give the P/C a moment to unwind, relax, calm down.

A handshake, a few kind words, and a moment or so of social interaction will melt the block and permit communications to flow more freely.

The "graduate handshake" is what I call the use of *two* hands instead of one. It carries twice the impact, delivers twice the warmth and sincerity.

The handshake can have psychological importance all out of proportion to the tiny effort it requires.

Non-verbal communication techniques are being studied by social scientists at the Esalen Institute in Big Sur, California. Adults who train there participate in simple physical acts to unleash emotional blocks, such as hugging, dancing, rolling down a hill —all in the interest of greater awareness through human relatedness and human interaction.

Now, I am not suggesting that you go to these extremes with your P/Cs. But I do want to point out that some effort is necessary on your part to begin to improve non-verbal communication with them.

You may be reticent about handshakes. The famous pianist Van Cliburn prefers to clasp his hands together in the traditional Indian sign of respect. For the same self-protective reasons, a surgeon might wish to avoid the handshake. Whatever your reason, avoid the handshake if you will, but don't avoid expanding your non-verbal communications.

Pull up a chair alongside your P/C and sit knee to knee, eyeball to eyeball. Or, be more demonstrative with your hands. Place a reassuring arm on a shoulder or give a confident pat on the back.

Your facial expressions also convey extra meaning to what you say or what you *appear* to be thinking. P/Cs watch your face, especially the eyes, the eyebrows, the curve of the lips. These features are constantly revealing messages, real or imagined, to the other person and are picked up by his built-in tuning system, all the more sensitive at times of emotional stress.

Doctors, for example, during extended treatment or examination procedures, are watched carefully by the concerned patient whose imagination can easily exaggerate the meaning of the slightest frown or arched eyebrow. To these practitioners we suggest: Take a "smile break" or brief rest period every so often. This can be just a few seconds to ease the tension of the moment. It will have a brightening effect on both parties, and P/Cs will reflect the happier, more relaxed expression.

What the non-verbal elements of communication express very often, and very revealingly, is the emotional side of the message—in either a positive or negative way. Psychologist Albert Mehrabian has devised this formula: *total impact of a message = 7 percent verbal + 38 percent vocal + 55 percent facial.* The importance of the voice in daily communication with P/Cs (including case presentation) will be discussed more fully in Chapter 12, "Your Tattle-Tale Voice and What It Says."

First-Day Program—Discover the power of positive, non-verbal communication. Do some one thing all day, like shaking hands as you say "hello" and "good-bye" to a P/C.

The Second Day—Humanize Your Practice
Through Verbal Communication

The educators and psychologists among you have already detected the ultimate purpose behind the six-day deal I have made with you. They know that a book cannot set off an automatic reflex. On the other hand, a learned reflex can be touched off by a book, providing the conscious centers of the brain are actively involved. An act must be performed, and then reinforced by continual performance. To make changes in daily behavior and routine takes more than the decision. It takes initial doing and follow-up doing.

I know that the professional man who tries the First-Day Program will want to carry the human relations unfoldment a step further. The Second-Day Program involves making some change in verbal communications—either your spoken or your written word.

The power of the word, as with gestures, can be activated in either a negative or positive direction. Sometimes that direction is subliminal and of apparently little significance.

There seems little negativity about the words "Waiting Room," but negativity is there. Nobody likes to wait.

"Reception Room" bears little positivity, but positivity is there. Everybody likes to be received. Words can mean the same but touch off quite opposite feelings.

For example, when you attend an out-of-town program or convention, does your telephone receptionist or answering service have a definite wording to explain your absence to those who phone your office?

The word "convention," while meaning one thing to professional people, means something quite different to the average person. To the uninitiated, it conjures up visions of men in funny hats, drinking and singing and having a whale of a good time.

To have it said that you are merely "out of town for the weekend" may leave the false impression that you are neglecting your practice and your patients or clients.

This is the view from the P/C's side. Hopefully, it will give you a new perspective, on a minor matter to be sure, but one that could have major consequences for your image and your practice.

How about having the receptionist say that you are attending "post graduate courses" or "continuing education," not for the purpose of impressing the P/C, but merely to inform him, in a *positive* way.

To put this perspective in clearer focus, turn it around. Suppose you called your accountant and learned that he was away taking some courses on the new tax laws. What could you really say, except "this fellow is on the ball; it's good to know he's keeping up to date."

A sailing enthusiast I know has named his boat "Consultation." When he takes an afternoon off, his receptionist explains to callers that "he is out of the office on Consultation." That, I think, is going a little too far.

There will be much more on harnessing the power of the positive word, written and spoken, later. But, as an initial personal involvement in the word game, it would be gratifying to you to see the immense effect that a few seemingly innocent niceties can have.

A mid-west photographer, successful as a portrayer of hard-to-take men, completes his verbal instructions, not with the usual command "smile!" but with the phrase, "now think of something pleasant." The result is a natural twinkle, instead of an artificial smirk.

Have you ever thanked an on-time P/C for being prompt? Those who do report less lateness.

Do you remember P/Cs (and families of P/Cs) by *name* and do you refer to them in conversation? Remembering peoples' names requires effort, but it's worth it. It's one of the many "little things" that evidences your sincere interest in the P/C.

The "trick" in remembering names is *incentive* and *determination*. The most complicated name or number can be remembered if there is a definite purpose or advantage and enough determination. Just left to "chance," without a deliberate effort on your part, it is natural for a name to slip away. Consider veterinarians who have to remember the names of *both* the patient (the pet) *and* the client (the owner). The successful ones do.

And the more successful and "important" you are, the more flattering it will be to those whose names you remember.

Make a determined start at remembering P/Cs' names. For just one day think of it as an experiment in improved human relations. When you see how really easy it is, and the elevating effects it has, you'll want to make it a daily habit.

Second-Day Program—Improve verbal communications with your P/Cs. Later chapters will provide specific verbal traps that lose P/Cs, and how to avoid them. Tested techniques will enable you to use verbal communications in your practice in a way that will make you wonder just how much of what you have said in the past was really getting through to your P/Cs, or getting through differently than you intended.

The Third Day—
Building Good Will (with Potlatch)

I first came across Potlatch in Governor's Harbor on the exquisite island of Eleuthera in The Bahamas. "Potlatch" was the name of a private club with service and facilities unsurpassed. Although rates were high, the difficulty of getting reservations attested to the enthusiasm of guests in paying them.

I was curious about the name "Potlatch" and discovered it is derived from an Indian expression meaning "I give you more than you give me." This philosophy encompasses a world of practice building. It is the distilled concept of humanizing professional relations. It is a fountainhead of good will.

A Pennsylvania veterinarian has a weighing scale in his reception area. Clients enjoy the opportunity to weigh their pets while waiting. And, of course, the information is useful in completing the case history.

A San Francisco practitioner, located on a high floor of a professional building overlooking San Francisco Bay, Golden Gate Bridge, and the city skyline, has floor-to-ceiling windows in his reception area. The breathtaking panoramic view creates a mood that puts people at ease. For those who wait, a zoom telescope is the perfect diversion.

A Los Angeles internist, thinking of his patients' comfort, uses *pre-warmed* instruments for internal examinations. Who wouldn't appreciate that . . . especially on chilly mornings!

An accountant in Eau Claire, Wisconsin, with a large number of once-a-year tax-time clients, sends out a quarterly newsletter that he writes himself summarizing tax law developments and calling attention to certain items by writing a personal note.

An attorney in Cleveland, Ohio, with a large divorce practice, has borrowed an idea from practicing psychologists. He lifts the cover of a box every time a feminine voice betrays the onset of tears—revealed is a container of tissues bearing the legend "Go ahead, you'll feel better."

A New England practitioner is an "honorary member" of Boys Town, the home and school for orphaned children in Omaha, Nebraska, founded by Father Flanagan. On the certificate, which hangs in his private office, is their "trademark" showing a small boy carrying another on his back and saying, "He ain't heavy Father, he's m' brother." He told me he displays it because he feels much the same way about his patients' need for warmth and the personal touch, and it isn't a burden to answer their needs.

This is Potlatch.

Potlatch is also the comfortable chairs, the hot coffee, the fresh flowers, the reception room comforts, and anything else that you can think of that puts people at ease, makes them feel at home.

Potlatch is giving P/Cs *more* than they expect, *more* than they are paying for, *more* than anyone else ever gave them under comparable circumstances.

Dr. Pearl Hauser of Detroit, Michigan, expressed it even more eloquently when she wrote me:

"Potlatch is Love . . .
Potlatch is having a new love affair with life each day . . .
Potlatch is a secret weapon, more powerful than the hydrogen bomb. . . ."

Third-Day Program—Try Potlatch. Think up one way of giving the personal touch to demonstrate your personal interest. There will be more on Potlatch later, but meanwhile make a start toward humanizing your practice by implementing one idea.

The Fourth Day—
Revitalize Through Environmental Control

Environment plays an important role in mood and feeling. People can be depressed or "lifted" by the office they work in. Industrial designers improve productivity for years to come in the buildings they create through their judicious use of light, color and form.

Can you picture the typical professional office of a generation ago? Doctor's offices had that clinical look: color schemes were hospital green or antiseptic white; furniture was styled in hand-me-down colonial. Lawyers' offices were noted for their cracked leather decor and the atmosphere was strictly cigar smoke.

Yet many practitioners have these offices today. They feel it necessary for their professional image, believing that any money spent for modernizing and decorating will be construed as "showing off" and proof-positive that "fees are too high." They fear that a "fancy" office will frighten P/Cs away.

However, according to our surveys, the public has quite the *opposite* reaction. They tend to resent the practitioner who refuses to invest in their comfort, convenience and care—especially if he drives a "prestige" car. It is an ironic example of an image that "backfires" when the P/C puts this interpretation on it.

Bare, drab, cluttered, or "strictly functional" offices affect both P/Cs and practitioners in a negative way. Often the reaction is unconscious.

Today, people tend to judge a book by its cover. They are apt to lose confidence in the up-to-date knowledge and professional stature of a man with out-of-date equipment and "second-rate" facilities.

A good looking office doesn't enhance a man's abilities, any more than good clothes do. But *to others*, it makes it easier to "appreciate" his abilities. Without other yardsticks of measurement, it often serves as his "credentials." There is more than a gram of truth in the saying: "The man who thinks, acts and dresses the air of success is more certain to achieve it."

"Environment" is part of that "air of success" and it can also affect the practitioner's *self*-image. It's hard to think and act with an "air of success" or sense of professional pride in surroundings that belie these feelings. If it becomes in any way "embarrassing" when friends, relatives or colleagues visit the office—if a practitioner feels "apologetic" for his office—the psychological effects of these self-image feelings alone can inhibit practice growth.

Going "first class" and *knowing* it's "the best" can be a tremendous boost for self-confidence and enthusiasm. It has provided many a practitioner with a "second burst" of practice growth.

Give the office a "new look" and the practitioner, his staff, and his P/Cs get an emotional lift from the modern, up-to-date surroundings.

Furniture can be reupholstered and rearranged; tattered or worn items can be replaced; art work or wall hangings can be changed, one room wallpapered, another's color scheme changed.

Items like telephones, typewriters and vertical files in decorator colors, an interesting lamp, an unsual magazine rack can initiate the process of exhilaration. Go the whole way—redecorate, remodel, refurnish, add an extension, build an entirely new office—and you open the floodgates of enthusiasm for yourself, your family, and your I-see-you-in-a-new-light P/Cs.

Fourth-Day Program—Make a change in your office. Get rid of something old. Add something new. Begin to improve your professional environment. Your practice is your best investment and will reward you manyfold.

The Fifth Day—
Humanize Through New Perspectives

Sympathy may be the door-opener to human relations; but, for a practitioner seeking ways to walk through that door, it is *empathy* that is needed. Sympathy lacks true involvement. Empathy, on the other hand, is the intellectual identification of oneself with another. It provides the insight, the understanding and the perspective that makes good human relations come about naturally.

It is not easy to put yourself in someone else's shoes and see his or her problems as he or she sees them. We get busy, behind schedule, sometimes totally involved with *our* work, *our* world, *our* point of view.

On this fifth day, let's take a moment to consider the P/C's perspective—the view, as we have said, from the other side. It will lend balance and harmony to our discussion of practice growth.

The Sioux Indian used to pray, "Great Spirit, help me to never judge another until I have walked many days in his moccasins."

Start "walking in your P/C's shoes." Better yet, if you are a physician or podiatrist take off your shoes and walk on the (tile?) floors, bare-footed. Pick a chilly morning.

If you're a physician, take off your clothes, don a dressing gown, and go into one of the tiny examining rooms and just sit. Look for something to read, or listen to your heartbeat with a cold stethoscope. Of course, I'd recommend that you do this "exercise" in empathy on a weekend, making sure the front door is locked and the shades are drawn.

If you're a dentist, sit in the treatment chair with cotton balls stuffed in your mouth. As you sit and salivate, imagine the patient's reaction, left to herself, while the doctor is in the outer office.

For any practitioner with a private office for consultation, sit in the P/C's chair—on the *other* side of the large mahogany desk. Look at the desk from the P/C's perspective. Is it "organized" or "cluttered?" What image does it project? What reaction do you get from the mood of the room? You be the judge—but be objective.

Sit in the reception room and appraise it in the same way. How is the color scheme, the wall decor or art? How is the lighting, the temperature, the seating arrangement? How would you rate the magazines? Is there an ash tray, a sign prohibiting smoking? Are there odors? If you were a *child* (and mother had brought you along), what would you do while she's inside?

Judging a book by its cover only, how would you rate this practitioner?

Evaluate your P/C correspondence and mailings by occasionally sending a copy of a P/C report, recall notice, policy letter, or monthly statement to *yourself*—at home. It will increase your objectivity and cause omissions, if any, to be more obvious.

Call your answering service and try to get hold of yourself. Pretend it's an emergency and see what happens. How does the privacy or protection, and how it is expressed, affect you—as a P/C?

I'll guess that those of you, who as patients, or clients, identify with these situations, are "rooting" for the others to take these empathy exercises.

The first time around, there are liable to be a few aches and pains, possibly a surprise or two, and most certainly a new perspective to consider.

Fifth-Day Program—*Take a cold, analytical, objective look at your own services, environment and policies from the P/C's point of view. Establishing new perspectives is the first step toward change.*

**The Sixth Day—Accelerate Growth
Through Attitude Management**

By the time the sixth day arrives, you will see how important a role attitude plays in every aspect of the re-humanizing of a practice.

Some practitioners suffer from "neophobia," fear of change. As a result, their office, their human relations, and their practice procedures do not evolve and progress.

One of the symptoms of the neophobic syndrome is attitude backlash. This is where the subconscious sends up smoke screens to protect the status quo. It begins to manufacture negativity.

Don't underestimate the power of negative thinking. It provides an unending source of "tested" practice-defeating ideas, pumping up reason after reason why the humanizing program will not work.

Negative thinking is the ability to focus on "shortcomings," the worse side of anything. It is a penchant for fault-finding and nit-picking. If there's a reason why an idea *won't* work, the negative thinker is sure to find it.

The etiology of it, for professional people, is apparent. Because of their background and orientation, they are trained, in a sense, to think negatively, to examine all the facts, to be cautious, to be safe rather than sorry.

Inherent in "problem-solving" is a consideration of the pros and cons of alternate solutions. In matters affecting the P/C's health, welfare and wealth, the "weighing of all factors" is both commendable and prudent.

However, in matters of human relations concerning the growth and development of your practice, this type of thinking can be dangerous if it stifles and holds back "change."

To be sure, *every* idea, procedure and technique has its shortcomings and limitations; there just isn't any foolproof, guaranteed method that will work 100% of the time. In baseball, we consider a .350 batting average as excellent, notwithstanding that 65% of the time the batter failed. It is a matter of perspective.

In our Phase I seminars, we often speak of "negative influences"—those factors that might inhibit or impede practice growth. We do so to anticipate those practitioners who will "see" these negative influences out of proportion to their size. We attempt to close off the escape hatches of rationalizing, regretting and procrastination—that tend to keep a practice "standing still" and "status quo."

Here, from post-seminar discussions, follow-up office visits, and surveys of countless practices of varying size, type and location, are ten reasons why a humanizing program "won't work," as stated most frequently by negative thinkers. The purpose is to put these "old reasons" (excuses?) in proper perspective and to recognize them for what they are.

1) ". . . my area is different." Areas *are* different, but the real difference that has the biggest effect on practice growth is one's *attitude* about the area.

A "low-fee" area can be blamed on the economy *or* it can be seen as a "low-appreciation" area that can be up-graded with proper P/C education.

A "slow practice" with limited referrals and growth can be blamed on the public's apathy *or* it can be viewed as an *opportunity* for success, with so much yet to be developed.

2) "*. . . my patients (clients) are different."* Consideration, understanding, appreciation and the other elements that humanize a practice work wherever there are P/Cs, because fundamentally people are the same the world over.

On many occasions I have seen a complete "turnaround" in P/C acceptance and practice growth following a change in ownership (or management) of a practice. The P/Cs obviously remained the same; only the methods of dealing with them changed.

3) "*. . . I don't have the time."* The little things that make big differences take no more than a few seconds or, at most, a few minutes. The "environmental changes," once they are installed, take no time.

4) "*. . . I'm too old to change."* I've met many septuagenarian practitioners at our seminars on practice improvement. They often take more notes, plan more changes than some of their younger colleagues. They seem to have more "fun" in their practice and keep youthful because of their enthusiasm for change. Their attitude is the antidote for that practice-stifling disease that Dr. Norman Vincent Peale calls "psychosclerosis"—hardening of the thoughts.

5) "*. . . The practice can't afford it."* Human relations are cost-free. Practice improvements in environment, facilities and staff aren't a "cost;" they're an "investment" in better service and practice growth. These changes can be programmed to fit any budget. Even $25 can begin to make a difference.

6) "*. . . I'll wait until I have . . . an associate,"* "more staff," "larger quarters. . . ." Human relations and practice improvements cause practices to grow. To hold back on these changes is putting the cart before the horse.

George Bernard Shaw commented, "People are always blaming their circumstances for what they are." Many practitioners have proven to me that we are the *creators* of circumstance, not the creatures of circumstance.

7) "*. . . I'm not the type."* Ever watch a magician perform? The tricks he does look so easy, until you try them yourself and discover you're "all thumbs." Learning comes with practice.

Human relations is like "magic" in more ways than one. It, too, is a skill and, like any skill, can be learned. The "trick" is just to start.

8) "*. . . My practice is satisfactory as it is."* Review the list of professional and personal goals in the Prologue. Perhaps one of these "refinements" will trigger additional interest. Practice improvement can be geared to any of these special needs and interests that may be deficient in terms of your long-range goals.

9) "*. . . That's not the custom among professional men in my community."* The urge to conform or "follow the pack" can stifle a practice, cause it to fall behind or keep it "average." If an idea makes sense to you, if it fits your professional objectives, ethics and abilities, and if you feel comfortable with it, it's worth a try. Why not lead your colleagues to a better way of doing things?

10) "*. . . I'm a professional man, not a business man."* Negative thinking compounded by the Ivory Tower Attitude can take one far afield. Practice improvement

is *first, foremost and always* better service to the P/C. Better service is not unprofessional. It begets referrals and prestige, which create income. When reinvested in the practice, income in turn provides better service.

Sixth-Day Program—*Analyze what "alibis" and "attitudes" are attempting to negate your natural desire for improvement. Recognize these ten roadblocks to change for what they are and reason them away. Fortify your desire to make changes for the better by bolstering your own positive self-image. Change the polarity of your practice from negative to positive by concentrating on the benefits of change, not the reasons "it won't work."*

THINKING MAKES IT SO

William James, dean of American psychologists, has said: "Man alone, of all creatures of earth, can change his own pattern. Man alone is architect of his destiny. . . . The greatest discovery of my generation," he said, "is that human beings can alter their lives by altering their attitudes of mind."

This wisdom applies to professional practice as surely as it does to our personal lives.

"Negativity" is, unfortunately, all too easy to manufacture about almost everything, including one's practice location, one's P/Cs, and one's potential for professional success. These "conclusions" can usually be supported by a long list of "reasons" and convincing arguments, especially if you look for them to "prove a point."

Worst of all, "negativity" has a tendency to become perniciously cumulative. The more negative reasons we find for resisting change, the more we refrain from doing anything about it and the more used we become to the "status quo." It then becomes even harder to change.

True to form, thinking *has* made it so.

There are always reasons for resisting change. The important thing is to see them in proper perspective. The president of the Gillette Safety Razor Company has this sign over his desk: "Nothing will ever be attempted if every possible objection must be first overcome."

How does one overcome "negativity?" Professor James had the answer to that too. Emotion follows action, he said. The best way to feel cheerful is throw your shoulders back, smile, and deliberately put a spring in your step. The best way to feel enthusiastic is to *act* enthusiastically, and the best way to develop a positive outlook is to take the *action-steps* that produce these emotions.

Any action-step that produces *change* will set in motion a "beneficient cycle" which causes one success to lead to another. It's like a snowball rolling downhill, getting bigger on each turn because it gathers more snow, and gathering more snow on each turn because it's getting bigger.

Start a list now of the action-steps you will make to start your practice-growth ball rolling.

3

Long-Range Practice Growth

Just as the technical side of practice is becoming more specialized each year, so is the management side of practice becoming more specialized, sophisticated, and important in terms of long-range growth.

Farseeing practitioners have recognized that one can no longer conduct a practice by guesswork or trial and error methods—on a day-to-day basis. Practice management by intuition, no matter how brilliant, has become a luxury even a flourishing practice can no longer afford.

In Dallas, Texas, the American Astronautical Society recently heard an address by Barron Hilton, President of Hilton Hotels Corporation. The subject? "The Lunar Hilton."

His opening remarks were, "Scarcely a day goes by when someone doesn't ask me, jovially, when the Lunar Hilton is going to be opened. They're joking, of course. But I don't see it as a joke at all."

He went on to describe some of the advance thinking and planning that has been done on this project, including the intermediary "Orbiter Hilton," which is already in existence! Known as the "Hilton Space Station Number Five," it was shown in a motion picture called "2001—A Space Odyssey."

His concluding comment was, "The method of getting a Hilton into orbit, or placed on the moon, though beyond our knowledge, is not beyond our imagination or ambition."

What makes the Hilton planning all the more visionary, is that the date of the speech was May 2, 1967, more than two years before man's first landing on the moon, on July 20, 1969.

Now, I'm not suggesting you begin planning for "moon practice," at least for the moment, but long-range plans for practice growth, well conceived and executed, are the first steps in realizing the attainment of your professional and personal goals, whatever they may be.

"QUALITY" VERSUS "QUANTITY" IN PRACTICE GROWTH

A primary decision, to be reached in the development of a practice as soon as possible, is: Should the *basic, underlying emphasis* of the practice be on "quality" (limited P/C volume with full-range services) *or* "quantity" (high P/C volume with limited [basic] services)?

A choice is necessary. A high-volume, full-range service practice is possible, but not likely. High volume, by definition, usually means that less time is devoted to each P/C which, with the same personnel, can only be accomplished at the expense of full-range services.

If you were to plot a graph of a growing practice, one that was reacting to a humanizing program, the result would be an upward curve rather than an upward, straight line.

An interesting fact about the humanized practice is that once growth starts, it begins to accelerate at a faster and faster rate. But, then, as more and more demands are made on the practitioner, it becomes likely that a point of diminishing returns is reached where the quality of service is forced to deteriorate as the quantity of P/Cs served continues to increase. This causes the rate of growth to taper off and possibly even to decline as referrals slow down and "drop-outs" increase.

All this does not happen overnight, of course, but many practices can be observed heading in this direction. People are "stacked-up" waiting. Telephones jangle. Personnel scurry back and forth. People come and go.

In the vernacular of some of the professions, this type of practice is called a "fire engine practice" or, as the dentists say, "drill, fill, and bill."

In an effort to speed up appointments and scheduling, some health practitioners have installed a system of coded lights above each examination room indicating P/Cs in various stages of treatment. Others have initiated "time and motion" studies with "time records," in an effort to extract the last drop of productivity from their time. And up to a point, of course, this practice-analysis is commendable.

Some practitioners attempt to solve the quantity problem by enlarging the office, hiring more personnel or working longer hours. This may alleviate some of the growing pains, but it does not stop growth. The curve continues upward and, sooner or later, something has to give.

Such was the case recently at the New York Stock Exchange where growth in transactions brought with it a volume of paper work that threatened to inundate the entire operation. The stock market began closing earlier than usual to catch up on bookeeping and office routine.

FIVE DISADVANTAGES OF A QUANTITY PRACTICE

To many practitioners who have not yet reached a problem-creating volume, the prospect of quantity development is, of course, still appealing. However, even these practitioners are well advised to recognize the inherent disadvantages of a quantity-oriented practice, so that they can head off its eroding effects before the curve of growth begins to climb precipitously.

There are five main disadvantages of a practice where the emphasis is on quantity as opposed to quality:

Disadvantage #1—As the quantity (volume of P/Cs) increases, the actual time spent with each P/C, of necessity, decreases. The only alternative is to add more office hours to the schedule. Although a possibility for some, the general escalation of the working day or working week is not within the concept of practice growth as presented in this book.

As time with each P/C is decreased, a dehumanizing of the practice can occur. The emphasis shifts to technical service. Both the practitioner and the P/C are deprived of discussion, interaction and communication. The total needs of the P/C, be they technical or psychological, are either glossed over or ignored. The total knowledge and skills of the practitioner are not brought to bear, due to the pressure of time. He might treat a problem, but overlook the "person" or preventive measures. He is no longer able to render a complete, in-depth, personalized service.

Disadvantage #2—When the scope of professional and personal service is curtailed, the quality and value of practice may decline. The P/C feels a void. His understanding and appreciation of his problem, and what is being done or should be done about it, is inadequate. The result is a lack of motivation to follow through on all recommendations and suggestions. This is reflected in such matters as future "maintenance visits," and certainly enthusiasm drops way below the referral level.

Disadvantage #3—A quantity practice soon takes its mental and physical toll of the practitioner. The practice that is operating at full speed and full capacity is a ruthless and demanding taskmaster. Most practitioners are not built for the pace, yet they become trapped by it. Time becomes the all-important commodity, and there is never enough of it.

Little wonder that they become exhausted and run down, at times short-tempered, impatient and harrassed, and even family life can deteriorate. For some, there is a continuous sense of frustration, of never having enough time to do things as thoroughly and proficiently as one is capable of doing.

P/C communications begin to bog down. Disagreements and misunderstandings become more frequent. Even his staff and his colleagues are not immune from this degenerative process.

Disadvantage #4—A "booked to capacity" practice leaves little time for emergencies and for seeing new P/Cs. The need to make appointments far in advance discourages newly referred P/Cs *and* referring colleagues. It all adds up to poor service and poor public relations.

Disadvantage #5—An overly heavy practice load leads to insufficient rest and relaxation and does not permit the practitioner to meet the constant demands for keeping up-to-date professionally. Weekends and holidays become engulfed in paper work, professional reading, and reports in a never-ending, "catching up" treadmill.

Many practitioners can function in this kind of an environment and still appear to be giving the P/C all the time in the world. They look unhurried and attentive and one would never perceive the pressure behind the scenes. Other practitioners who are hurried and harrassed look it.

In either case, the practitioner has the best of intentions. He is dedicated and motivated by a genuine desire to serve. He is rather the victim, not the villain, of a quantity practice.

HOW TO ADJUST THE LINE BETWEEN QUALITY AND QUANTITY

Professional growth often means slowing down a practice. The over-burdened practice will respond to this in quality and depth of service and, therefore, in referrals, prestige and income.

The slow-down process becomes one of doing the greatest professional good for the most people rather than doing the good that time will allow for the most people. The difference is perhaps more a matter of degree than kind.

In planning the growth and development of a practice, where you draw the line between a quality and a quantity practice becomes a matter of prime importance. The answer is not an easy one, for it depends on many factors and varies for the individual. The answer can often be found only in the *doing*. A quantity growth is encouraged to where the point of diminishing returns in depth of service rendered is recognized.

For the practitioner who wants to slow down his practice, two methods are available:

1. Limit the practice to P/Cs who appreciate top quality professional services, weeding out those who do not want or will not accept this type of service.
2. Raise fees.

These alternatives should not be selected arbitrarily nor initiated without a concomitant change in some other aspect of the practice. Obviously, the practitioner whose approach to P/Cs has, for one reason or another, failed to educate them on the availability and desirability of complete service, must revitalize that approach. Just as obviously, a higher fee structure without a commensurate rise in the level of service can boomerang.

Subsequent chapters on attitude management, the dangers of the Ivory Tower At-

*titude, and humanizing techniques are considered as prerequisites to any action de-
signed to quality-orient a practice.*

With that in mind, let us examine the approach that might be used in each of the
two quantity-slowdown methods.

HOW TO GRADE YOUR P/Cs' SERVICE I.Q.

Although we constantly speak of a "practice" as though it were a homogeneous
unit, it is in actuality a heterogeneous "group of individuals." Before we can limit a
practice by weeding out less than desirable P/Cs, we must distinguish between basic
types of P/Cs.

For simplicity's sake, we can divide P/Cs into four categories, representing different levels of understanding and appreciation of complete professional services
(Service I.Q.). These can be labeled *A, B, C, D.*

"A"—These are the well-informed type, who fully understand and appreciate your
professional services and what you are trying to do for them. They are well-motivated,
cooperative, and an enthusiastic source of referrals.

"B"—These are similar to the "A" group, but informed and motivated to a lesser
degree.

"C"—Their service I.Q. and follow-through is on the borderline between procrastination and consent. They require prodding, reminding and, above all, P/C
education.

"D"—This group has the lowest service I.Q. In every sense, they are marginal
P/Cs and are the logical prospects for the quantity-slowdown process.

These ratings are not based on formal education, standard I.Q. measurements,
social standing or economic status. Ironically, in many cases, their service I.Q. may be
inversely related to these factors.

Although all practices have some of each category, you might say a "quality"
practice is composed *primarily* of "A" and "B" types, while a "quantity" practice is
predominantly "C" and "D" types.

Let's examine further the makeup of the "D" group.

FIVE TYPES OF LESS-THAN-DESIRABLE P/Cs

It should be made clear then in considering the "less-than-desirable" category of
P/Cs, we do not equate them with the "slow-paying" or "delinquent" type of P/C,
although slow-paying P/Cs frequently prove to be undesirable for other reasons. Their
delinquency is generally a sign that they do not appreciate the practitioner and the
quality of service he is performing. It could be that some "slow-paying" P/Cs are less
than desirable for this reason alone.

In general, I have found that practitioners in all fields recognize five basic types
of P/Cs who do not measure up to the image of an ideal P/C:

1. P/Cs who are "no-shows." They cancel, change, arrive late, or not at all. This is a consistent pattern with them and is usually without good reason.

2. P/Cs who want service for the immediate problem only. These P/Cs understand emergencies but cannot understand the value of complete and preventive service, despite repeated efforts by the practitioner at education.

3. P/Cs who do not follow instructions. They seek advice but, when they get it, they do nothing about it. They have no follow-through.

4. P/Cs who do not accept the authority of the practitioner in professional matters. These are the P/Cs who argue, debate, and challenge the practitioner's opinion.

5. P/Cs who are apparently emotionally volatile or neurotic. These are the over-talkative and over-demanding, who expect more time and attention, either over the telephone or in person, than the case justifies or that the practitioner can give.

These five types of P/Cs contribute liberally to the inadequacies of a quantity practice. Lack of understanding and lack of appreciation lie behind their lack of desirability as a P/C. There is nothing involved here that P/C education could not correct, and I repeat: Before any P/C can be considered less than desirable, he should be given the time and opportunity to learn the facts in the due course of practice, using a down-to-earth, humanized and concerned approach set forth on the pages ahead.

THE TWO PREREQUISITES FOR INCREASING FEES

The subject of fees, especially "high fees," is a delicate and controversial matter in these inflationary times. The implications and consequences are far-reaching.

As with many of the other "sacred cow" subjects presented in this book, the purpose of the discussion is to give you new perspectives, food for thought, and alternatives from the world of professional practice, from which you can determine your course of action.

Since the reasons for holding fees "in line" are well known, let us turn our attention to some of the positive aspects of increasing fees, especially as they are related to "quality" of service.

But first, and as prerequisites for increasing fees, there are two important premises:

1) In order to raise fees, a better service must be offered:

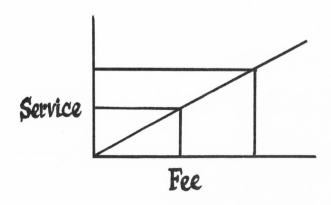

Since most practitioners are undoubtedly offering first-class technical services, the greatest opportunity for improvement lies in extra-technical dimensions—avenues such as better environment, improved facilities, more time with the P/C to listen, explain, educate, motivate and other personal interaction.

2) In order to raise fees, an improved attitude of self-worth must be adopted:

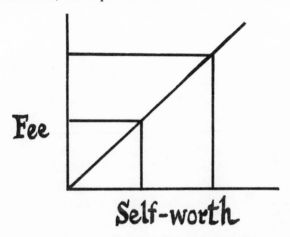

Of course, fee is also based on knowledge and skills, as well as the attitude of self-worth. But we are assuming that, as a college student, every practitioner has acquired the knowledge in abundance and, through experience, every practitioner has developed his skills to a high level. With fees based on three factors—knowledge, skills, and self-worth—and with two of these relatively fixed, then the only variable left to adjust is self-worth.

How does one establish his self-worth?

Is it the "going rate" in the community? Well, it's certainly a good starting point but actually it only represents what *others* think *they* are worth. The urge to conform may be necessary for many reasons, not the least of which is the law itself or some other "third party" regulation.

But assuming there is freedom of choice, part of each person's worth is determined by P.M.A.—Positive Mental Attitude. You are worth what you think you are worth.

A negative mental attitude, representing a feeling of limited self-worth, creates a consciousness of limitation that psychologists tell us acts as one of the greatest deterrents to success. It acts as a "self-fulfilling prophecy." When it becomes a low-fee consciousness, it perpetuates a low-fee practice.

FIVE FACTORS TO CONSIDER BEFORE RAISING FEES

Raising professional fees is not the risky and critical step that many practitioners see it as, yet it requires sober thought prior to a decision.

There are five clear-cut factors that bear on the problem:

1. Is a higher fee structure in the public interest? More specifically, will the reduction in P/Cs served be counter-balanced by the increased service possible to those who remain? By limiting the number of P/Cs, higher fees enable the practitioner to do

the best work of which he is capable. He has the time and opportunity to consider the total needs of his P/Cs and to *prevent trouble* instead of just *coping with it.* Less pressure keeps the practitioner in better condition mentally and physically. It permits him to keep up to date professionally. He is able to give more of himself—to P/Cs, family, community—and there is more of himself to give. As a byproduct of higher fees, a better income will enable the practitioner to re-invest a portion in his office, equipment and furnishings. He can hire capable assistants. This all contributes to quality of service.

2. Do higher fees lead to a public image of being material-minded? Some practitioners who have earned the reputation of being "money-mad" might have failed to justify a higher fee structure through a more complete, in-depth, personalized service.

3. Will a higher fee structure decrease *professional* referrals? Once again, the burden of justification is on the practitioner. If he is willing to give "problem cases" the extra time and attention that busier (referring) practitioners are unable to give, he will be recognized and appreciated. Their enthusiasm will be a source of many additional referrals which will insure a steady source of enlightened P/Cs.

4. Will higher fees seem "expensive" to P/Cs? If they do, can P/Cs be frightened away and become carriers of a distorted, "high-priced" image of your practice? The answer to a large extent will depend on how your fees are presented and explained to the P/C (see Chapter 10).

"Average" fees seldom affect a public image. "Higher-than-average" fees do affect a public image. But let us examine that effect. (Remember though, we are talking about a thorough and personalized professional service.)

"He's expensive, but he's good." Is this image dangerous? Certainly not in the healing arts, and certainly not in matters fiduciary and financial. This image can enhance professional stature. It can build P/C confidence. It can even make advice more "valuable" and treatment more effective.

Many practitioners report that better fees frequently produce better results for the P/C.

In the absence of other criteria, a professional fee is often interpreted by a P/C as a "measurement" of a practitioner's ability and reputation. P/Cs paying a higher-than-average fee will often assume that they are getting better-than-average care and advice. This is a positive reaction; it is also a valid reaction. The way it works out is that they are usually correct.

Harry M. Fain, noted California attorney and Chairman of The American Bar Association Section of Family Law, has written: "We cannot expect the public to have professional confidence in a lawyer practicing family law who cannot maintain adequate office facilities; or who cannot maintain himself or his family with an adequate economic basis. Nor can the public maintain confidence in a lawyer who undercharges or fixes fees without relation to nature, difficulty or importance of the work he performs. This is neither sound economics nor good ethics. Under-evaluation of services is just as unprofessional as over-charging." *

---

* Harry M. Fain, "Fixing Adequate Fees in Domestic Relations Cases," *Family Law Quarterly,* June 1968, published by The American Bar Asociation Section of Family Law.

5. Will a high fee structure cause a P/C "rebellion?" Some present P/Cs will probably "drop out" or "switch." If this thought is undesirable or unbearable, than maybe a fee increase is not for you (see Chapter 11 however for a different perspective on this matter).

But, if you are willing to accept the inevitable loss of some P/Cs, especially those in the less desirable "D" catagory, the rewards will be more than compensatory in the resulting better informed, more receptive, and more cooperative and enthusiastic category of P/Cs that will characterize your practice.

An Arizona practitioner decided on a 20 percent increase in professional fees and lost 8 percent of his clients. It takes only simple arithmetic to determine his net gain in time and remuneration.

Note: None of the foregoing should be considered as in conflict with doing charity work, donating free clinic time, or contributing in some other professional way to the community. Nor is fee raising intended to be directed at special, individual cases where you feel a reduced fee is warranted because of a P/C's need for service and the inability to pay for it. In fact one of the benefits of attaining a successful practice is that it enables a practitioner to be more generous and charitable with his time and talent; he can more easily afford to do so than the practitioner who is struggling to "make ends meet."

EFFECT OF FEE ON PROFESSIONAL SELF-IMAGE

Higher fees provide monetary income to be sure, but even more importantly they provide what behavioral psychologists call "psychic income." They can have a positive effect on self-image, yielding a source of pride, self-worth and ego-fulfillment which in turn is felt by P/Cs through increased confidence and enthusiasm.

There are notable exceptions of course in the areas of education, research, social work and government, to name just a few fields where dedicated professionals are engaged in public service.

But for a professional person engaged in private practice on a fee-for-service basis, the matter of fees and practice income can affect his self-image, his attitudes, and even his performance, subliminally. For example, to whatever extent a practitioner feels "underpaid" for his time, skill and knowledge, it can plant the seeds of resentment towards his work and ultimately his P/Cs.

A weak self-image saps enthusiasm and resentment can destroy it. This negativity interferes with and impedes the growth and development of a practice.

This self-image matter may seem trivial, but in my travels I've seen many occasions when a higher fee structure has changed and strengthened a self-image, diminished resentment towards time-consuming services, and was the catalyst for tremendous practice growth.

Of course, to raise fees for the sake of raising them, or for the purpose of bolstering one's sagging ego, is open to justifiable criticism. The way it actually works out is that, as practitioners increase fees, they invariably work harder for P/Cs. They more willingly and cheerfully give a more complete, thorough and personalized service.

Are their efforts prompted by a desire to justify the fee or ease one's conscience? I rather think they are a natural outpouring of enthusiasm—enthusiasm for self, work, profession and P/Cs.

MORE PRACTICE GROWTH—WITH LESS VOLUME

Where income is basically derived from time, skill and knowledge—as in most professions—the formula for that income is:

$$\text{Volume (P/Cs)} \times \text{Fees (per P/C)} = \text{Income}$$

There are four combinations possible to reflect how a single practitioner might utilize his time:

$$\text{High Volume} \times \text{Low Fees} = \text{Income}$$
$$\text{High Volume} \times \text{High Fees} = \text{Income}$$
$$\text{Limited Volume} \times \text{Low Fees} = \text{Income}$$
$$\text{Limited Volume} \times \text{High Fees} = \text{Income}$$

The first two reflect the quantity practice, the last two the quality practice.

Two of these formulae eliminate themselves. A limited volume combined with low fees is possible, but not desirable. A high volume combined with high fees is desirable, but not possible. (By definition, high volume precludes thorough professional and personal services. Since "time" is a component of "fee," this combination dictates lower fees, all other things being equal.) So, by elimination, the practitioner is faced with a choice between:

$$\text{High Volume} \times \text{Low Fee} = \text{Income}$$

and

$$\text{Limited Volume} \times \text{High Fee} = \text{Income}$$

On the face of it, the choice seems to be six of one, half a dozen of the other, but let's take a "real life" example and see what really happens:

A practitioner in Ohio had for many years maintained an "office visit" fee schedule of $4.00. Two years ago he had the following volume-fee-income statistics:

Patient Visits	Fee	Gross Income
9,500	$4	$38,000

He had the usual hesitancy and reluctance about raising fees, but decided the time was right to make a change. Here is what happened the following year:

Patient Visits	Fee	Gross Income
8,900	$5	$44,500

Yes, he lost patients—600 of them—but, in so doing, he was able to work at a slower pace because of the "time saved" with "limited volume." (At fifteen minutes a visit, it amounted to 150 hours during the year or three hours a week.) He was able to give remaining patients a little more time and attention, with less "pressure," and still had more time for himself and his family. (His office expenses also decreased because of less bookkeeping, paper work, etc.) The $1.00 increase in office-visit fees resulted in these benefits *plus* an increase in income of $6,500!

Food for thought: According to statistics from practically every national association I've seen, if only *half* of the public was to receive *half* of the professional service and attention they *now need*, their members couldn't handle the traffic, let alone keep up with the continuing needs of the future. The loss of some P/Cs therefore, is not as serious as it may at first seem, especially if it results in better care and improved services for those remaining.

The more serious problem is of course the "manpower shortage" that exists in many professions. The prospects of attaining a more successful, less taxing practice (than current conditions permit) may be one answer to student recruitment.

VITAL STATISTICS
EVERY GROWTH-CONSCIOUS PRACTITIONER SHOULD KNOW

Our Ohio practitioner who raised his office visit fee from $4 to $5 would have had to lose 20 percent of his patient volume before he incurred a loss of income from the previous year.

Can you believe that a $1 increase in fees could cause a loss of 20 percent of P/C volume? For this to happen, something else of a much more serious nature would have to be wrong for P/C confidence and trust to be so easily shattered.

At a base fee of $5, an increase to $6 would require a loss of almost 17 percent to break even; from $6 to $7, a loss of almost 15 percent; and from $7 to $8, a loss of almost 13 percent—still more attrition than should be expected from a $1 increase in fees.

Note: This particular range of office visit fees has been used as an illustration because it is so common among healing art practitioners. The principle, however, holds for any type of practice, any fee schedule, and enables one to determine, statistically, the gain or loss effect of changing volume and fees.

HOW TO RAISE FEES PAINLESSLY

Most practitioners are faced with the need to raise fees even if only by reason of spiraling costs. I have watched many struggle with the decision. They discuss the pros and cons at length with their families and staff. They compare their fees with "national averages" and with their colleagues. They deliberate and debate with themselves— "Should I? . . . or shouldn't I? Will my patients (clients) accept it . . . or won't they?"

It often takes a couple of years for the fee increase to materialize, finally triggered by an accountant, a seminar, or the knowledge of what a college classmate is charging.

And after all these mental gymnastics, what finally happens when the new fee schedule goes into effect? Usually nothing. It's a day like any other day.

Because of infrequent visits, many P/Cs do not even notice an increase in professional fees. Those who do, usually accept it as a matter of course, an economic fact of life. Percentage wise, the complaints are few and far between, causing most practitioners to wonder why they worried and waited so long.

Once you've decided to raise fees, what's the best way to do it? Send advance letters to P/Cs? Post an announcement in the reception room? Allow a "grace period?"

There is a two-word formula for raising fees painlessly that's been thoroughly tested and proven by countless practitioners in many varied fields? It is simply—"Do it!"

It is *not* a life-and-death decision. It is not an *irrevocable* decision. Although I have never seen a practitioner regret or reverse his decision to increase fees, there is the option, if necessary, of readjusting fees (and service) to the former levels.

A week or two should suffice to test this new approach to practice. Prepare to be surprised. Despite expected losses, many practitioners and referrals report that, following an increase in fees, they *get busier*—more referrals than ever. When all the forces and factors we have been talking about come together in the right combination, there is a synergistic effect.

Here, in summary, are the reasons why practitioners' volume actually increases:

1) In charging more, these practitioners also provide better service, more time and attention to each P/C, better facilities, equipment, and decor.

2) These practitioners are more enthusiastic about their practice, their P/Cs, and themselves. These feelings are contagious.

3) People often assume because something costs more, it's better.

At our seminars, I ask groups, "What effect, if any, has a higher fee structure had on your practice?" The answers, of course, vary; but it is very impressive to an audience (and precisely the reason that we ask the question) when approximately 20 percent of the practitioners report they have become busier, their volume increased.

And those are the statistics.

Time and time again, I see higher fees = better service = exuberant practitioners = enthusiastic P/Cs = greater income = office improvements = better equipment and decor = more referrals = greater success. It seems to be a time-honored economic law: Success begets success.

HOW LONG-RANGE PLANNING
SIMPLIFIES PRACTICE MANAGEMENT

Earlier we posed the question: Should the *basic, underlying emphasis* of the practice be on "quality" or "quantity?" The philosophy of each, as we have shown, is different. More importantly, the day-to-day management, even the furnishing of each type of practice, is different, and in some respects totally divergent.

For example, office location and parking facilities can be "adequate" or "above-average."

Professional equipment, furniture, and office machines are available in a wide range of quality and price, new or used.

Carpeting, drapes, lamps and a host of other decorating alternatives and optionals are available in different qualities and at different prices.

Stationery can be "offset" or "engraved."

What is the "proper amount" to be spent in these cases?

The quality-oriented practitioner, by definition also needs the "best of everything" and doesn't hesitate to order it, or replace it when needed. His quantity-oriented colleague must think and buy differently—for many reasons.

A quality-oriented practitioner, like his business counterpart, would rather be over-staffed than under-staffed. His philosophy demands it. His fee structure makes it possible.

And there are many other considerations. How about office hours (and days off), appointment-scheduling (time allowed per P/C), progress reports and follow-up visits, continuing education, professional entertaining, and certainly many personal, Potlatch services for the P/C?

How about the "calibre" of outside advice in matters of accounting, law, insurance and investments?

All these decisions can more easily be resolved, once the basic character and philosophy of the practice is established.

The following excerpt, from a recent ad by Merrill Lynch, Pierce, Fenner & Smith, Inc., illustrates how long-range planning establishes standards for practice management, service and personnel:

WHO WANTS TO BE AVERAGE?

It was G. K. Chesterton who wrote that the hardest thing in the world to be was exactly "average."

Which could be true.

But in our business, who wants it?

Average service? Average facilities?

Average personnel?

You'd be out of business in no time.

Because people invest money to make money. As much money as they possibly can, consistent with their own financial situation—the risks they can afford, the rewards they seek.

So nobody we know wants an average broker.

Or average help, either.

That's why we accept only 1 out of 25 applicants for our training school—put them through the most grueling course we know of in our business.

That's why we spend more than four million dollars a year to maintain what we honestly feel to be one of the biggest and best research Divisions you can find in the investment field.

That's why fourteen Merrill Lynch floor brokers work out of nine strategically located booths on the New York Stock Exchange, each one of them handling only about 125 stocks so that they really get to know the market for these stocks.

And that's why we pioneered in electronic computers—constantly keep looking for new ways to speed orders and confirmations and increase the efficiency of all operations for the benefit of our customers.

SUMMING UP

The management alternatives for long-range practice growth appear to be a choice between doing the greatest professional good for the most people or doing only the good that time will allow for the most people. At the two extremes, it is a choice between *complaint* care and *complete* care.

Strong arguments could be made for both types of practice. Indeed both types of service are necessary to suit the tastes, needs and limitations of both the public and the professions. In a non-controlled, private practice, the choice between the two depends on your "philosophy" of practice, your professional objectives, and your answers to the following questions:

To whom do you owe what?

Do you owe your P/Cs the best of your training and ability, or a compromise?

Is it better to *prevent* trouble or *cope* with it?

Is it better to have fewer but *convinced* P/Cs or many but *confused* P/Cs?

Do you prefer the "best of everything" or will "second-best" suffice?

Are longer hours and crowded schedules in the best interests of your P/Cs, your family and yourself?

Action-step: As a guideline to practice development, many practitioners have found it helpful to *write out* their answers to these questions, to *crystallize* their "philosophy" of practice—on paper, and then to *verbalize* these long-range plans and objectives with their associates and staff, often with the P/Cs themselves.

4

How to Reach New Heights
in Professional Success

The white line you see on cargo ships and many ocean liners is called the Plimsoll mark, after the British statesman Samuel Plimsoll. It indicates when a ship is being overloaded. If a load is too heavy, it causes the ship to sink past this line and indicates that the ship is in trouble.

In many respects, a professional practice is like a seagoing ship. It can be built to custom specifications, cruise at any speed, carry any load. There are many alternatives.

Professional practices have Plimsoll marks beyond which knowledge and skills are submerged, forward momentum is reduced, and practice growth is stifled, and a practice that has sunk below its Plimsoll mark is also in trouble. Unlike a ship, however, this Plimsoll mark is not readily visible or easily recognized.

The purpose of this chapter is to help you find the Plimsoll mark for your practice and, in doing so, to make the changes that will accelerate the growth of your practice —to reach new heights in professional success.

THE PLATEAU OF PRACTICE GROWTH

The general growth pattern of many professional practices appears as follows:

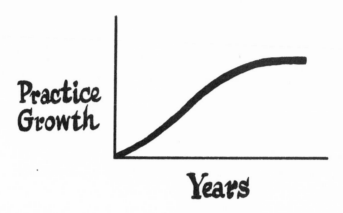

For the first few years of practice, the young graduate is bursting with enthusiasm, a concern for his P/Cs, and a determination to succeed. His P/Cs, few and far between at first, are given the best of professional and personal services, and they are pleased and refer their friends to him. His efforts produce slow but steady practice growth.

The initial growth pattern of most professional practitioners is similar. It is in later years that the differences occur.

For many, a slowing-down process occurs after eight or ten or twelve years—to be sure, at different levels and rates and to different degrees. For some, a leveling-off occurs, resulting in a "plateau of practice growth." And for a few, an even more serious change occurs, causing what one consultant describes as "practicide"—where practice growth actually diminishes.

Controlled practice growth is certainly commendable and desirable, especially in later years. It is, of course, the unplanned and unwanted changes and reductions with which we are concerned.

What then causes these premature slow-downs in practice growth?

Is it a "saturation of service" in the community? Possibly, but not likely, especially considering the current population explosion and increasing demand for professional services. In fact, I have seen practice slow-downs occur in some of the fastest-growing communities in the country.

Is it because these practitioners have reached the "limits" of their time and abilities? Again this is a possibility, but I have also seen many "booked-to-capacity" practices begin a whole new pattern of practice growth, a *"second*-burst" as it were, once they have found the key to unlock their growth potential.

In our studies of professional practices, these slow-downs in practice growth seem to occur most frequently because of restrictions and limitations imposed by the *practitioner himself*.

In some cases, they may be the effects of "diminishing returns" from a high-volume, quantity practice, as described in Chapter 3. The personal service and attention, the thoughtful concern and countless "extras" that were freely given to P/Cs in the early days of the new practice are slowly eliminated as volume increases, not always intentionally but because of the pressure of "time." As a result, referrals diminish and may even be offset by the attrition due to "drop-outs" and "switching."

It is perhaps ironic that in some high-volume practices, the very things that produced success in the early years are forgotten and discarded. As complacency sets in, practice growth and P/C referrals are taken for granted. A slow-down, in such cases, is inevitable.

Another factor that can cause a slow-down in practice growth is a "lack of change" in procedures and environment. The effects in this case are psychological and almost imperceptible. Daily routines, once interesting and challenging for these practitioners, tend to become monotonously repetitive with the passage of time. Slowly and unnoticed, such practices tend to become "stale," losing the warmth, sparkle, vitality, and ultimately the referrals and rate of growth of earlier and more enthusiastic years.

"Boredom," although seldom admitted as such, is often the underlying cause and it can, and does, happen even in the most "dynamic" of profesional practices. It often explains the appeal and attraction of outside interests such as sports, the stock market, even sideline businesses—to the point where they begin to interfere with the practice itself.

These changes in outlook are not unique to the professional world. They can happen in every walk of life and every type of business.

They occur for those who have reached their Plimsoll mark.

ATTITUDE MAKES THE DIFFERENCE

In Chapter 1, two basic attitudes were discussed: the "Ivory Tower Attitude" (ITA) and the "I Care Attitude" (ICA). The difference, and it may only be a matter of degree, can determine if a practice is standing still, just plodding along, or moving "full steam" ahead.

Let's see, at the two extremes, how ITA and ICA practitioners view various situations in day-to-day practice. Which come closest to your feelings?

Situation	Ivory Tower Attitude (ITA)	I Care Attitude (ICA)
Practitioner self-image	Authoritarian, aloof cold, distant with P/Cs.	Warm, friendly, down to earth with P/Cs.
Professional services	Technically-oriented.	*People*-oriented.
Practice growth	"Practice-building" and "making money" are selfish motives and incompatible with the ideals of professional practice.	A successful practice provides more and better *service* for more people. Greater income is a byproduct of a successful practice.

Situation	Ivory Tower Attitude (ITA)	I Care Attitude (ICA)
Office decor	a) An office that is "functional" is good enough. It is only a means to an end. b) Detained P/Cs sit in "waiting rooms."	a) An office that is functional *plus* aesthetic, pleasant, and up to date improves service and morale. b) Detained P/Cs relax in *"reception* rooms."
P/C education and motivation	a) "Selling" and "high pressure" tactics are unprofessional and undignified. b) "Quality care" is limited in a low-fee area.	a) Helping the P/C understand and appreciate the benefits of complete care is a professional obligation. To ignore this phase of practice is a disservice to the P/C. b) Quality care is *unlimited* in a *low-appreciation* area. Low-fee areas don't exist.
Fees	Stated on a "take-it-or-leave-it" basis.	The P/C is *entitled* to a discussion and explanation of all fees.
Referrals	a) Taken for granted. b) Satisfied P/Cs send referrals.	a) taken with *gratitude*. b) Enthusiastic P/Cs send *more* referrals.
Staff	"Lay help" working for the practitioner.	*Professional assistants* working *with* the practitioner.
Public Relations	Commercial and self-aggrandizing.	a *Service* to the community and the profession at large.
P/Cs who procrastinate and "drop out"	Practice failures are blamed on area, colleagues or P/Cs themselves.	Practice failures can be solved by *feedback* and *change*.
Changes in procedures and environment	"Status quo" is best.	*"Progress"* is a challenge and an obligation.

These small differences in attitude can make a big difference in practice growth—in terms of service, referrals, prestige and income.

Let me say again that the Ivory Tower Professional is not a villain, but a victim. I have never met a practitioner who deliberately, purposely and consciously adopted an Ivory Tower Attitude. The onset of ITA is so gradual and natural that many never realize they have it. The real villains, if indeed they can be called that, are the ever-increasing demands of a high-volume practice and keeping up to date. These require, of necessity, a *technical* orientation and one that all too often excludes the humanized dimension and "I Care Attitude."

Maybe you're not an Ivory Tower Professional. Very few practitioners are, in the pure sense. The fact that you are reading this book is a good indication that you do have a strong "I Care Attitude."

But, to whatever extent ITA exists, it is an inhibitor of technical ability and a deterrent to practice growth. So it has a built-in, self-perpetuating mechanism that resists change. The only way it can be removed is to understand it thoroughly, to see it in new perspectives, and to be aware of its alternatives. Only this understanding can build up a motivation for change.

HOW TO RELEASE PRACTICE-GROWTH POTENTIAL

How does one change a pattern of behavior that has become ingrown over the years as a well-established habit, even a way of life?

Can it be done quickly?

Can it be done at all?

The electronic age has taught us how to program the most sophisticated computers with accuracy and almost lifelike results. Now man is learning how to program the human mind—the most sophisticated and versatile computer of all.

The process, when self-applied to the mind, is seldom called programming, but rather "attitude management" or "auto-conditioning." Properly conditioned, the mind drops old, unwanted attitudes and assumes, as a new habit, the desired attitudes.

The process of conditioning oneself consists of three basic steps:

1. See old problems in new perspective.
2. Understand the desirability of change.
3. Have a determination to change.

The turning point is change. And, once the change is made, the new attitude ingrains itself each day as a habit. The programming is completed. Under the influence of the new attitude, the mind ceases to hold back practice growth and, instead, becomes a "direction-finder" for attaining professional and personal goals.

ATTITUDES, ABILITIES AND SUCCESS

"Ability" is 100 percent of success at professional school, but far from it in private practice. Unlike the university professor, the P/C cannot judge your ability. He has no way to recognize, evaluate or appreciate it.

Research made a few years ago by the Carnegie Institute of Technology included an analysis of the records of 10,000 persons. Their conclusions were that, even in such fields as engineering, about 15 percent of one's financial success is due to technical ability and about 85 percent is due to personality factors, including attitude, human relations and the ability to communicate!

Although knowledge and ability are, of course, important, they serve no purpose and have no value until they are *applied*—for the P/C's welfare.

Thus, the transition from professional school to private practice requires a change in perspective.

We have said that the professional man in the world today has a dual responsibility and obligation to his profession and to his P/Cs.

1. He must keep up to date professionally and use this information to determine the needs of his P/Cs.

2. He must gain the acceptance and cooperation of his P/Cs so that a program offering maximum P/C benefit will be implemented.

The first is really the technical ability to *diagnose*—to discover the problem.

The second is really *communication*. It is the necessary link between "discovering the problem" and "solving the problem"—between "knowledge" and the "application of knowledge." Schematically:

By definition, the Ivory Tower Professional, who has the technical abilities to correctly diagnose the P/C's problem and subsequently to solve it, is not really contributing to his welfare until he can *communicate* the facts and gain P/C acceptance. His knowledge and skills, superior though they may be, are "inert" until the P/C agrees to follow through.

Is this perspective building up an appetite for change? Can there be any more professional reason for changing ITA than to further your own professionalism? You just cannot top that.

You can see the purpose of the Six-Day Program in Chapter 2. It has helped many to begin the process of change.

Step 1—Toward New Perspectives

The Ivory Tower Practitioner looks upon the education and motivation of P/Cs as "selling." It bothers him and appears in conflict with his professional role.

The word "sell" is from the Anglo-Saxon and, in its original form, it means to "deliver," on a mutually acceptable basis. The word did not originally include pushing, forcing, or applying high pressure. It connoted enlightening, informing, and communicating relevant facts.

And is there anything professionally wrong with that? No matter what the profession, its goals are advanced when its practitioners become skilled in overcoming P/Cs' human nature to procrastinate, rationalize, or find an excuse to delay action!

Let's use some examples from everyday practice. Let me ask you to become a "third party," and judge for yourself the "ethics" or appropriateness of a few, specific examples.

Example 1

Heat-treated (break-resistant) spectacle lenses are available for opthalmic prescriptions. They are slightly heavier and thicker and do cost more than "ordinary" opthalmic lenses. They are not readily accepted by patients.

Question: How "persistent" and "persuasive" should the practitioner dispensing these lenses be with a "monocular" patient—a child, or an industrial worker in an occupation with potential eye hazards? How much "initiative" and "time" should the practitioner take? Should he "bang" the glasses on the table (if necessary) to demonstrate their impact resistance? Should he emphasize the "peace of mind" that patient (or parent) will have knowing these lenses are "safer?" Should he point to a "Sight-Saving Citation" awarded to him by Bausch and Lomb Optical Co., saying, "whose use of impact-resistant lenses has prevented eye injury or possible blindness in the case of an accident experienced by (name of patient and date of accident)"? * Should he point out the danger of wafer-thin, "ordinary," brittle glass being one-quarter inch from the eyes, especially since much thicker, plate-glass was outlawed for automobiles many years ago?

What are the ethical limits of persuasion in this case? Consider a speech made in the U.S. Senate on August 2, 1968, by Senator Warren G. Magnuson of Washington, where he reported: "The 500,000 eye injuries suffered each year by Americans, and more than 161,000 of these are children, could have been prevented or, at least reduced in seriousness if the victims had been wearing protective eyewear."

Example 2

How much "reminding" and "urging" should a lawyer give his client relative to the following five reasons for having a will and reviewing it periodically?

A. The client, instead of the courts of the state, can name the executor and may excuse him from furnishing an expensive surety bond.

B. The client, instead of the state, can name the guardian for a minor child or incompetent heir.

C. The client can create trusts for his heirs for various purposes and reasons to prevent needless dissipation of his assets.

D. The client can minimize the amount of taxes involved against his estate.

E. The client can provide for gifts and bequests to his college or other worthy associations.

Example 3

How far should a veterinarian go in "reminding" clients of the need for re-immunization against distemper or other diseases? You be the judge of a letter from a client † who was not so reminded.

To the Editor
Modern Veterinary Practice
American Veterinary Publications, Inc.
P.O. Drawer KK
Santa Barbara, California

Dear Sir:

Just a few weeks ago, we lost our 9-year-old Poodle, who died with distemper. And my brother lost his Cocker with the same disease.

We have had Poodles since 1937, and each has had the normal series of protective shots when a puppy. As far as I knew, this immunization was good for life.

Because of the expense of bathing and grooming Poodles, we probably see veterinarians more often than most people do. BUT NEVER IN ALL THESE

---

* Offered by Bausch and Lomb Optical Co., Rochester, New York, to practitioners submitting documented case histories of such events.

† "Modern Veterinary Practice," December 1965; Reprinted by permission of the publisher.

YEARS has a veterinarian told us that dogs should have "booster" distemper shots from year to year.

Therefore, it is my feeling that veterinarians are grossly careless in this connection, and it is my hope that through your publication you can and will remind them that it is their duty to inform dog owners of the necessity for three shots.

Since we lost our dog, I have talked with many people, and none of them has ever heard of any immunization shots, other than the puppy series.

This information needs to get to the people, and it will have to get there through the veterinarians. I hope that this letter will help, in some way, to save other dog lovers from the sadness we are experiencing.

Thank you for your attention.

Very truly yours,

Mildred C. Chambers

Mildred C. Chambers

Example 5

How do *you* feel, *as a patient or client* in a professional office, about the following:

—waiting beyond your appointment time?

—receiving a substantial bill with the only explanation being—"for professional services?"

—getting "rushed through" your appointment?

—waiting rooms that look like "waiting rooms?"

—practitioners who are "authoritarian and aloof?"

At our management seminars, we will frequently use examples from varied professions to permit practitioners to view their attitudes from new perspectives. It is easier to draw conclusions and form opinions when one is at the receiving end of professional services. Shortcomings are more obvious and viewed differently. The full impact and consequences of ITA are felt.

Step 2—Understanding the Desirability of Change

The prospect of change is seldom greeted with open arms. Our hostility toward it ranges from simple procrastination to outright obstinacy. All of nature has this resistance to change—it is called *inertia*. So it might be said that it is natural to resist change.

However, it is unnatural to resist *forcibly*. In nature, trees sway with the changing winds and it is usually the brittle tree that is first to succumb.

If something is inhibiting communication and human relations, the finger of blame must ultimately point at some aspect of the Ivory Tower Attitude as the basic cause.

Remove ITA and your potential for practice growth assumes its proper level.

Replace ITA with ICA and the change ignites the potential for continued practice growth. It becomes growth activity.

To resist such a change, to hang on to ITA, is to deny your profession the expectations it has of you. It is to deny your P/Cs the expectations of a complete, in-depth, personalized service they both want and need. And it is to deny your family and friends the joy of a glowing, expressive professional.

Many practitioners understand the desirability of change. They have the potential for continued practice growth and the insights and ability to do it, but something else stops them at this critical stage of their career. It is procrastination.

The plateau of practice growth is the fate of those practitioners who neglect to follow through on their early momentum.

These practitioners are not failures; neither are they successful. They go so far and no further. They have good intentions. They make plans for "change" and continued practice growth—perhaps their own professional building, new equipment or office decor, a larger staff or an associate—but they never quite get around to doing anything about it.

It has been said that procrastination has no advocates but a lot of friends. We admonish P/Cs for it, but seldom ourselves. Bruce Barton, famed advertising man, said it rather succinctly when he wrote of "wasted years": "In almost every life there are some fruitless years; but the tragedies occur when year after year men go along feeding their lives to the locust of indecision, the locust of laziness. . . ."

There is also the locust of ITA.

Step 3—How to Overcome Attitude Inertia

The antidote for procrastination is simple:

Men who are *determined* to change and improve usually accomplish their purpose. They see their practice growth potential in clear perspective and understand the desirability of change. Their conviction for change is strong enough to overcome inertia. Their "secret" is persistence. It combines patience with determination.

Often their progress is so rapid it surprises even them.

They find, to their amazement, that the difference between an "average" practice and an "above average" practice is relatively small, that it requires only a *little more* effort in order to go a *lot further,* just as a man has to be only a few inches taller than others to stand out in a crowd.

"Nothing in the world can take the place of persistence," said Calvin Coolidge. "Talent will not; there have been many unsuccessful men with talent. Genius will not; unrewarded genius is almost a proverb. Education will not; the world is full of educated derelicts."

Talent, genius and education can flicker into oblivion without the flares of persistence.

SYNERGISTIC EFFECTS OF
ATTITUDE AND ABILITY

What happens to practice growth when the Ivory Tower Attitude is changed and a more humanized ICA is adopted? Attitude and ability have been mentioned as separate characteristics. Indeed, they are separate to the extent that someone can have a great deal of technical ability and any attitude, from ITA to ICA, or vice-versa.

Yet, as determinants of practice growth, attitude and ability, in fact, reinforce each other and act as synergists.

A humanized ICA "multiplies" a practitioner's technical abilities. It induces maximum motivation to learn more from his P/Cs, from his colleagues and instructors, and from books, journals and courses. His broader perspectives and receptivity to change enable him to see "meaning" and "application" in many ideas that others pass by and gloss over.

He is stimulated by the challenge of change in professional technology, equipment, environment and communication. He has more "fun" in his practice and is more *enthusiastic* about his work, his profession, his P/Cs and himself.

And he reaches greater heights in professional success because *enthusiasm,* as I have observed, is the world's *second* most contagious feeling.

What is even more contagious? I think it is a *lack of enthusiasm.* Be it a yawn, boredom, fault-finding or negativity, it spreads like wildfire to P/Cs, to staff and to colleagues and, just as surely, ravages practice growth.

Thus, there is a dynamic relationship between "attitude" and "ability." It takes a combination of the two, each working to reinforce the other, each having a "multiplier" effect on the other, to insure practice growth.

These characteristics, remote as they may at first seem, help to explain some incongruities in professional success. We see the practitioner who is highly competent and technically proficient, yet who has achieved only mediocre practice growth, if indeed any at all. Then, at the opposite extreme, we see the practitioner with good, but still "average" technical skills, who has achieved immense practice growth.

It's the "multiplier" effect of *attitude* that makes the difference.

ATTITUDES AND ALTERNATIVES

For some, success is a destination, a goal to be attained. Actually when you stop and think about it, success is the whole journey, not just the end of it. It starts with the first step toward success and continues with every other successful step. It's like going on a vacation. Much of the fun occurs in the planning, anticipating, packing—long before you get there.

In reality, success is a state of mind. The successful practitioner thinks in terms of "I can." His less successful colleague thinks in terms of "I can't." It's a way of looking at life.

I remember a college professor who always kept a drinking glass on his desk, upside down. Whenever a student expressed a negative attitude, he would walk slowly up to the tumbler, pick it up in his hand and exclaim, "What a peculiar drinking glass; it has no mouth." Then, lifting the inverted glass, he would peer underneath. "And the bottom is gone."

A lagging practice can often begin to spurt ahead when the attitude of the man behind it is turned around. Here are some attitude reversals. I call them the Attitude Miracle Makers:

From *ITA* to *ICA*.
From *I ought to do that* to *I will do that*.
From *I don't give a darn* to *I care*.
From *don't bother me* to *it's no bother*.
From *I do what I can* to *how can I do more*.

CHANGE AND CREATIVITY

The beauty of change from the ITA to a humanized ICA is that you can be entirely yourself in going about it. You can be just as free in how you do it as you were free in adopting ITA characteristics.

There is no prescribed behavior pattern. You express creatively your new attitude. You are yourself. Being yourself is being creative. I will give you hundreds of examples of what others do, but you should do what comes naturally.

In the Six-Day Program of Chapter 2, I described the broad categories in which you would be creative, but I hope I inspired you to "do what comes naturally" in these categories.

Human creativity is the ability to bring things or concepts into being that have not existed previously. There are dramatic examples in the arts; but in its broadest meaning, creativity refers to the power to originate in all spheres of human activity—including, or perhaps I should say especially, human relations.

Describing the "Creative Force," the German composer Richard Wagner wrote, "I am the secret of perpetual youth . . . from the rock whereon I light, new life begins to flow . . . I . . . create a fresh new existence."

Create your own change. Show concern for your P/Cs as people in your own creative way. Communicate it. Begin your own fresh new professional existence.

5

Setting the Stage
for Practice Growth

"There'll be a change in the weather. . . ." The lilting melody of the popular song of a few decades ago goes through my mind when someone asks where to begin the process of change towards a P/C oriented practice.

". . . From now on, there'll be a change in me," went the song's lyrics.

The change is an inward change, and how it manifests itself is up to the individual.

Some of the changes have absolutely nothing to do with practice management or the new humanized dimension, at least initially. One practitioner told me he changed the ink in his fountain pen to green. To him, it meant "go." A podiatrist started jogging. An architect began to start his day earlier. An accountant told me he started by ordering a custom-made suit. "It made the change to a quality-oriented practice official," was the way he explained it.

You can make it "official" in your practice in any number of ways. The first step, although seemingly unimportant at the time, frequently turns out to be the beginning of a chain reaction, as one improvement leads to another.

Most practitioners find that a few simple changes in office environment and decor are not only easy to implement but are also quickly noticed by P/Cs. The results, in this way, are immediate.

Here is a sampling of practitioner ideas, gathered from office surveys and seminar feedback, that have produced positive results for others. Some will be more applicable or appealing than others. Adapt, change, refine, improve to give them your "personal touch."

LITTLE TOUCHES THAT TURN PEOPLE ON

The inception of change need not be heralded by a blast of Joshua's trumpets that send the walls of your office tumbling down to make way for a complete remodeling.

It can start with an illuminated globe, or a fish tank, or old apothecary jar filled with hard candies, or a color telephone.

These are the touches that turn people on. They reach people. They affect you and they affect me.

Color reaches people instantly. It is stimulating to the senses. We react to colors. Red is particularly stimulating. Even the appetite is affected, as most restauranteurs know. Hence the red walls, red ceiling, red tablecloths, and red carpets in many successful restaurants.

It is no coincidence that red is associated with the Fourth of July, Christmas, and Valentine's Day. It excites patriotism, religious fervor, and romantic emotions. It is also a danger signal, especially indicative of emotions that are out of control.

Yellow light is said to appeal to people in the realm of the intellect and intuition. The ancients wore yellow amulets as a protection against disease.

Green is nature's color. Psychological tests find it to be a tranquil color that neither excites or subdues. It is refreshing, relaxing and healing.

Blue is associated with sky and water. The ancients considered it as a symbol of truth. Emotionally it inspires peace. Tests have found it to be the most soothing and subduing color. It has a way of inducing thought and deliberation. The violet and purple range of the blue spectrum can have an elevating (royale) effect or, in their weaker shades, a melancholy effect.

Colors can make you happy, cheerful, or gloomy. Brillant hues are agitating. Pastels are pacifying, especially in those blues and greens.

It is better to have color than no color. It is better to bring brightness and drama into your office than have it just lie there—dull and "turned off." If you are truly interested in P/Cs and their emotional needs, you cannot help but be interested in re-examining color in your office from the viewpoint of psychological effects.

Flowers bring color and, along with it, a liberal injection of cheer for P/Cs and staff. Everyone enjoys fresh flowers and the happy thoughts they convey. If your garden can't stand the drain, arrange with a local florist for weekly delivery. A physical therapist I know receives them fresh every Monday morning and, at the end of the week, takes them home to his wife. Even a bud vase with a single flower can brighten a room.

The choice of flowers, fresh cut or planted around your building, also makes a personal impression. Morning glories, petunias, tulips, and daffodils are types that everyone knows; they create warm, friendly feelings. More formal planting or specimens of rare plants create a different mood, a serious feeling.

Here are some more examples of those small touches that create warmth, interest and individuality.

1) Musical chimes in place of the standard doorbell or telephone ring.

2) A mobile or piece of sculpture add interest and distingué to any office. Today, original art can be purchased at modest prices, rented from a local gallery, or perhaps placed in your office "on loan" from a local artist or P/C.

3) Attractive lamps can provide just enough color accent and decor to change the polarity from drab to interesting. Many objects can be electrified, thus creating a one-of-a-kind accessory of added interest. I recently saw a lamp made from a cobbler's last with a shade decorated with designs of high-laced boots. It fit perfectly in an office of early American design.

4) Create a "gallery" of framed antique maps, documents or interesting photographs. They can be of historical interest or P/C interest. An Iowa dentist's "No Cavity Club" of childrens' photographs is a delight to his little patients and their parents.

The fountainhead of ideas is endless and many afford a good way to start the change to a warmer, more attractive office—quickly and inexpensively.

READING MATTERS

The late Raymond Rubicam, founder of the advertising firm of Young and Rubicam, was one of the most creative and effective advertising and public relations executives of all times. His personal motto was: "Always resist the usual."

The usual professional office looks like it has been visited by the usual magazine subscription salesmen. It has the same popular magazines that one finds in the usual offices and the usual homes.

How about some that are unusual—to keep P/Cs' minds and eyes off the clock?

Some alternatives: Consider, in addition, an assortment of some interesting, less frequently seen magazines. *Punch,* the English equivalent of *New Yorker,* for example, is novel in this country. Its sophisticated commentary, low-key humor, superb cartoons, schedule of London's cultural events, even the advertising, make fascinating reading for the waiting P/C.

Or join the British Magazine of the Month Club and receive a different magazine direct from London each month. The clatter of Soho and the quiet of Scottish moors; Old Vic and Saville Row; the wit of Parliament and the mod madness of Liverpool—they will all be there.*

That will be a change.

Others that I have seen in professional offices, and that people enjoy reading for

---

* For further information, write British Magazine of the Month Club, 545 Cedar Lane, Teaneck, New Jersey, 07666.

a change, include *Realities, Scientific American, Venture, Horticulture* and *Psychology Today*. The list is endless.

A number of interesting booklets on educational horizons are available from the National Education Association in Washington, D.C. They will be glad to supply a list.

Or subscribe to a museum art bulletin. Many major city museums include this with membership.

An Oregon practitioner subscribes to newspapers from Around the World,* a different paper every other week, printed in English, from such exciting, exotic and important places as Athens, Hong Kong, and Saigon. Needless to say, his clients appreciate a glimpse of the world through the eyes of the *China Mail, Jerusalem Post, East Africa Standard, Manchester Guardian* and the like. And their appreciation focuses directly on the practitioner.

This type of reading material is a compliment to your P/Cs' interests as well as a refreshing change from the ordinary.

Another interesting item you might want to add to reception room reading material is a colorful, illustrated cookbook. Add a pad inside with the words, "for making notes" and watch it eat up waiting time.

Or add picture books of art, antiques, or architecture.

Or a copy of the 1908 Sears, Roebuck mail order catalog. It has recently been reprinted by the Follett Publishing Company of Chicago.

Unusual magazines and books not only give your P/Cs something interesting to read, but also something different to *talk* about on social occasions. Is it remote to think that your office may be mentioned in the course of conversation related to an article the P/C was reading? Odd as it may seem, some referrals do get started in this roundabout way.

In any event, the thoughtful selection of reading material for your reception room is nothing more than taking a personal interest and concern for P/Cs during times when they must, unfortunately and perhaps unavoidably, wait for their appointment.

The "unusual" costs no more.

TELEPHONE TIDBITS

Instead of putting incoming telephone calls on "hold" while records are checked or information is obtained, how about this alternative? Install a taped music system into the telephone so that callers will get pleasant music from Broadway shows. For P/Cs at the other end, it makes waiting a little more tolerable and assures them that they are still connected. You know only a few seconds can seem like an eternity when you are holding a silent telephone receiver. These attachments can be rented from the phone company in some parts of the country.

Another "people pleaser": How about a telephone, "pay" or otherwise, that P/Cs can use for outgoing calls? If a P/C is kept waiting and has to make a call, say to rear-

---

* For further information, write Readers World Press Club, 7 Delaware Drive, New Hyde Park, New York 11040.

range *her* schedule and other appointments, it's understandably pretty infuriating if she is not permitted to use the office phone. If she is allowed to do so, there's no reason she should feel guilty about an extended phone conversation with a friend. A thoughtful convenience, such as an extra telephone, is one way of saying "I care." And the alternative, as always, seems to say, "I don't give a damn."

SITTING PRETTY

Did you ever "peek" into the reception room and notice how people are seated? Studies have shown that men and women have definite, but different preferences.

Men, as a rule, prefer to sit cross-legged. When given a choice, they will select a chair *with arms*. Seated in this position, the body's center of gravity shifts off center, and leaning on the arm of a chair maintains a comfortable balance.

Women, as a rule, prefer to sit "straight-legged." Accordingly, when they are given a choice, they will select a chair *without arms*. It is more natural and comfortable for this position.

Older people, especially those with arthritis, find that low seats are difficult to rise from. Given a choice, they prefer a higher seat.

As strangers to each other, people tend to avoid sitting together on a couch, especially a love-seat. It forces proximity. Given a choice, they will select a chair.

Are these hard and fast rules? I doubt it, but having waited in many a reception room and having spent many hours "people-watching," I find these "rules" pretty consistent. Take a "peek" yourself; see if this isn't so. If you find I'm right, provide an assortment of chairs for the varied preferences of your P/Cs.

POTLATCH FOR CHILDREN

Children are visitors to most professional offices, either as P/Cs themselves or because Mother doesn't have a baby-sitter.

The idea is to keep them busy, out of mischief, and out of your staff's hair. Give 'em something to do and the problem will be solved. Toys, coloring books, "magic slates," a rocking horse, building blocks, their own little furniture or unusual reading material. Parents appreciate these items and your concern. It spares them the added burden of supervising their children, especially when they are not, at the moment, feeling up to it.

Other waiting P/Cs will also appreciate the peace and quiet. (Other people's noisy children can be quite disturbing.)

Here are some other ideas. How about an "Ant Farm?" It's a plastic anthill, completely enclosed. It's filled with sand and frisky ants, digging tunnels, building bridges and running about. There's even an executive-desk version for grown-ups.

A practitioner in Houston has a separate, scaled-down reception room just for children. No big people allowed. It has a nautical theme, a captain's wheel, a ship's lights, and at children's eye level, two ship's portholes through which the kids can see tropical fish swimming in the "ocean." (The aquarium, in this case, is located on the other side of the reception room wall in the back of a closet.)

Many practitioners put an old typewriter in the corner of the reception room. Children love it.

How about a View-Master with stero slides of cartoons or faraway places? One practitioner includes educational messages in the slide series.

Or a giant, stuffed Panda? Let the children name it.

A Maryland practitioner bought a potted palm tree from a display studio for the children's corner. By adding a few toy animals, he created an engrossing "jungle" and unusual conversation piece.

Your reception room need not be a playground or entertainment center but neither should it be a dismal and depressing "waiting room."

In treatment rooms, some dentists use a miniature TV (with earphones) for children to watch during routine procedures. One southern practitioner told me he even schedules children, when possible, during their favorite daytime program. Grown-ups seem to prefer recorded music, which he also offers.

What a "change" from the fear-producing environment of yesterday's dental offices.

The practice-growth importance of these "extras" for children is not only that they are practical ways to keep "little hands" busy. In a more subtle way, they "announce" that you do treat children, perhaps as a specialty. You'll find that many a parent, perhaps not realizing this before, will inquire further. It might result in a new patient. Regardless of your motive, these ideas can work for you.

"Rewards" for good behavior are standard procedure in most offices that treat children. Balloons, rings, and other inexpensive novelties are the usual "prizes." Here's an alternative:

A successful Georgia practitioner, Dr. Vernon Brabham, makes a "check-up" an "adventure" for his little patients. At the conclusion of the examination, they go to a specially designed and decorated "treasure cove," complete with pirate's chest and wall mural. From it, they select an authentic reproduction of ancient coins dating back 2900 years. Included with each is a brief history of the coin.* As he explains, "I provide this little extra, firstly because I genuinely like kids and secondly, because it makes for good patient-relations."

For the successful practitioner, Potlatch isn't an effort. It's fun.

Many practitioners "set the stage" for their children P/C visits by having their assistants send an informal note to the child in advance of the appointment. Personal mail makes every child feel "important."

For these notes, an Ohio dentist uses a long, narrow pad form with a colorful giraffe extending the full length of the paper. His secretary includes a reminder about the appointment time and adds: "We'd like to know more about you, so think of something special to tell us or show us, when you visit." It is an example of personal attention, above and beyond the call of duty, that paves the way for rapport and friendship.

Summed up, the alternatives to the care and handling of children, as well as all P/Cs, can be either ITA or ICA.

---

* For catalog of ancient coins, write Creative Concepts, P.O. Box 6297, Marietta, Georgia 30060.

TRICKS WITH LIGHTING

Professional offices generally need light-conditioning more than they need air-conditioning. An office can be lifted above the commonplace with light. Light can breathe life into dead colors and enliven dull corners with sparkle and interest. P/Cs respond with a new and brighter outlook.

Practitioners are not immune either. Brightness has a way of converting negativity into positivity. It literally illuminates the dark areas of office doldrums and transforms them into areas of stimulation. By and large, I find successful practices have a higher level of illumination for people and about people.

Lighting today is largely concealed and built-in. Recessed fixtures, coves, pin-hole spot and valance lighting provide the aesthetic beauty of illumination without the cost of an unattractive fixture.

General office or reception room lighting is best accomplished by indirect lighting where the light source is hidden and the ceiling and walls act as a reflector or indirect source. Dark ceilings and walls are poor reflectors. They absorb lighting. One fixture, strategically located, and a smooth white ceiling, will brighten a room sufficiently for general purposes.

Specific purposes must have their own light source. These are lamps or spots at reading locations, treatment areas or desks.

Fluorescent light sources are six times as efficient as the incandescent light sources. Did you know that a 15 watt fluorescent tube will produce 900 lumens compared to the 138 lumens of a 15 watt bulb? However, the bulb will prove far more effective when a strong beam of light is required for a localized area.

DECORATING ALTERNATIVES

During a recent lecture tour, I visited the offices of a midwest podiatrist whose practice, he said, wasn't growing as he thought it should be.

One aspect of his practice-survey concerned the office decor, which I noticed was curiously done in dark, bold masculine tones and style. I say "curiously" because in podiatric practice, it is a rule of thumb that 80 percent of patients are women. I asked if this was true for his practice and he agreed it was. I then asked why the decor was so masculinely oriented.

He said that he hadn't really thought about it as such, and didn't have an explanation. The decor, it seemed, was more "by accident" than "by design" and further suggested that he was more "podiatry oriented" than "people oriented." This outlook became more obvious as our discussions proceeded.

Part of his practice improvement program included a change in the reception room decor with emphasis on the "feminine touch." The black leather chairs were replaced with upholstered ones in bright fabrics. Blue carpeting was ordered with coordinating drapes and wallpaper. The level of lighting was increased and a vase of fresh flowers was added. Women's fashion magazines were placed in the physiotherapy rooms.

Months later, he wrote me describing the effects of the "new look" in his office. It amounted to: "I never realized that decor could make such a difference. The feedback from patients has been terrific. Even my staff has perked up." The tagline was: "The first month we showed an increase of 17 percent over last year."

Obviously it wasn't only the "new look" in *decor* that made a difference in morale and practice growth. It was the "new-look" at *people* which made itself felt in all phases of the practice.

You may not have bad breath, but do you have bad taste? It too can lose friends and influence practice growth and no one, not even your best friend, will tell you about it.

The percentage of women P/Cs in other professions may be less. However, there is value to the feminine touch in any office decor. It is the same as the homelike touch. And everyone appreciates that.

I have seen the homelike theme carried all the way in a reception room, right to and including a fireplace, a rocking chair, a bookcase.

We have all seen the magic that draperies can work. Window treatments can set the stage for a variety of decorator styles: Queen Anne, English Regency, Victorian, Spanish, French Provincial, Colonial, Modern—you name it.

Once named, follow through on that window style in the selection of furniture, coverings and carpets.

The results should be harmonious. Achieve a blend of compatible textures and styles, but not to the degree that boredom sets in. You need a yellow pillow, or a red lamp, or some other accents to the general theme.

Today, interior designers advise to "mix" rather than "match." They say to mix styles, finishes, colors and woods, as long as the end result is more harmonious. It is said to be more interesting.

An alternative to do-it-yourself designing is to hire an interior decorator. These professional people are well-informed about styles, color, values. They will help you to express your own taste and preferences and add a "professional touch" that will enhance your office.

The important consideration is not who designs your office, but that it is designed. The P/Cs feel the difference. They feel the personal concern of the practitioner for their pleasure, comfort and sensibilities.

The practitioner and his staff will also feel the difference in their "home away from home."

MOOD ELEVATORS FOR YOUR STAFF

Environment affects peoples' moods, personalities and outlook, for better or for worse. The psychological effects of color, office decor and "little touches" reach not only the visiting P/Cs but, just as importantly, the staff itself.

Work gets done faster, more efficiently, pleasantly, and with more pride when the surroundings are people-oriented rather than just "functional."

For the receptionist who spends several hours a day on the telephone, even the design of it can be important. Some of the new styles and colors in phone equipment have helped to solve the problems of "telephonitis" in a busy office. For example, the new push button phones, the kind that emit a musical tone with each number, are a change from the ordinary. They're even kind of fun to use and women appreciate the fact that, unlike old-fashioned dial phones, they don't ruin their manicures. A phone that's pink or blue and lights up, has an added brightening effect.

Make a present to your receptionist of a telephone in her choice of color and style. It'll be a good investment. The gesture alone will be appreciated.

Typewriters in decorater colors and contemporary design (perhaps with beige or blue typing ribbons) and elegant, engraved stationery (with matching inks) can also have a mood-elevating effect on written communications.

For women office assistants who wear white uniforms, a change to "color" can be a real mood-elevator for everyone. A starched, white uniform, although traditional, does soil easily, magnifies the tiniest spots and wrinkles.

Many health-care practitioners have renounced the usual "hospital white" uniforms for their staff, noting the negative psychological effects they have on children, on adults too, and even on the assistants themselves.

Soft, pastel colors are flattering to most women and are therefore nicer to wear. Many office assistants have told me that, following a change from the standard white uniforms, they have received many P/C compliments. This certainly results in a "perking up" which is radiated back to P/Cs.

Although some practitioners have expressed the concern that colored uniforms are associated with beauty shops and coffee shops, I've never talked with a patient who thought so. On the contrary, they say these colorful fashions are "less official" and friendlier.

Here's another area for change. How about converting some storage space to a "staff room" with refrigerator, hot plate and a couch for snacks, rest or relaxation? Even a minute or two away from the rush and hustle of a busy office is enough to revive the spirits.

You'll find that "fringe benefits" become "P/C benefits" when your staff's mood is elevated.

CARPETING FOR COMFORT

Carpeting has a place in professional offices. More and more it is becoming the standard. Even veterinarians report that their patients have less "accidents" because of the conditioning associated with "house-breaking" and the assumed responsibility that owners take in controlling their pets in a carpeted area. The same seems to apply to cigarettes and mud.

In treatment rooms, the last stronghold of tile flooring, doctors are finding that new carpeting materials are stain-resistant, look better, are easier and less costly to maintain, and most importantly, feel better to walk on—especially for bare-footed patients.

To be extra safe, some practitioners have installed loosely laid carpet squares, any one of which can be replaced if necessary.

Another variation is electric carpeting. Called Diolen, it consists of polyester fiber interwoven with copper electrodes. It can be set for a desired temperature and will radiate heat evenly. Using little electricity, it provides comfortable heat at low cost.

How about carpeting *outside* the office? In Huron, South Dakota, a practitioner has red, outdoor carpeting extending from the doorstep of his professional building to the sidewalk. Year around, it is a warm and friendly "welcome" to his guests. It is an outward sign, literally, of "rolling out the red carpet" for his visiting V.I.Ps.

A Philadelphia practitioner reports that the blue-carpeted steps in front of his brownstone office, on a street with similar homes, makes it easier for clients to find his office.

A Florida dentist I know installed carpeting on the *ceiling*. That's right. He carpeted the ceilings of his treatment rooms in pale green. As he explains, it has proven to be an effective ice-breaker for the new patient and a relaxing distraction and diversion during treatment. For the "captive" patient, it's a welcomed change from the usual, plain plaster ceiling.

To add further interest, he also placed a small shelf a few feet from the ceiling— at perfect eye level for the patient in a reclined dental chair. On it is a colorful figurine and bud vase of flowers. This patient-oriented doctor had obviously considered his patient's perspective—physically and psychologically.

A Texas podiatrist adapted this idea by installing wallpaper on the ceiling of his treatment room. The pattern he chose was "Footprints."

RECEPTION ROOM MAGIC

The reception room is apt to be the most active spot in any office. Any time, effort, or money you invest in making it comfortable and charming will reap dividends for years to come. It also reveals worlds about you, so it pays to put your best foot forward.

A "decorator trick," where budgets are tight, is to splurge in one small area. If you can't afford, for the moment, to go "first class" on an entire room, concentrate on one corner, or even one item. Invest in one really nice decorator accessory—a lamp, a wall clock, a mirror, an oil painting. It will be the focus of attention and tend to distract from the less important furnishings.

Even a beautiful crystal flower vase or ash tray will do the trick. And the best of these can be purchased quite inexpensively.

Gaining widespread popularity in recent years for informal reception areas are the so-called summer furniture sets. You can furnish an entire room with handsome rattan or wrought iron chairs, tables and occasional pieces that are suitably casual in feeling, easy to care for, and so light in weight that they are easily rearranged.

Accessorizing the reception room provides a real opportunity for self expression and the personal touch. Let good taste be your guide and refrain from being too whimsical or too obvious. Model sailing ships, a brass American eagle, wall plaques, decorative tiles, copper accessories—these are the kind of accessory ideas that may supplement the basic theme of the room.

The reason so many offices look uninspired today is that so many practitioners buy the same things and use them in the same way. Originality reflects imagination, thoughtfulness, depth of character.

The alternative is somewhat bland by comparison.

BIG IDEAS FOR SMALL RECEPTION ROOMS

Small reception rooms are the rule rather than the exception. But the economies of the situation are unappreciated by P/Cs sitting knee to knee or shoulder to shoulder. Here are some ways to make a small room seem larger:

1) A large mirror conveys an illusion of depth to the smallest room and it is appreciated by women who want to "freshen up" when entering or leaving. (Some practitioners have provided an alcove with vanity table, hand mirror, box of tissues, etc., for this purpose.)

2) Scenic wallpaper with outdoor scenes seems to push back the wall, taking the eye down a garden path or along a quaint street. Only one wall needs to be covered with scenic paper while other walls can be painted or papered to match its background color.

3) Coordinating floor and wall treatment provides an optical illusion. Unbroken lines are more pleasing to the eye and give the feeling of more space in a small area. Choose a light or neutral tone for flooring; then have the walls and ceiling painted to match. Parallel lines will also guide the eye into seeing more than is actually there. For example, inset strips of woodgrain into the floor; then continue them on up one wall.

4) To make a small window seem larger and to increase the size and importance of any window, hang curtains from the wall on either side, framing rather than covering the window itself.

5) Color can make a room seem larger or smaller. Warm hues in which red or orange predominate give an illusion of being closer than cooler blues. So you can move your walls back and separate your furniture by keeping decor predominantly recessive blue.

BULLETIN BOARD BENEFITS

A Colorado Springs practitioner installed a cork bulletin board in his reception room which includes, among other items of patient interest, the following announcement:

"I will be out of the office from time to time this year while attending post graduate courses. These programs make it possible for me to keep abreast of the many technological changes occuring in our field and to bring new and improved methods back to my practice and the patients I am privileged to serve. You realize that I could not undertake this advanced study if patients like you did not give me encouragement and assistance, and I thank you. For any emergency, please contact the office as arrangements have been made to have someone care for you."

Then he posts the actual program announcements including the list of topics and course descriptions. It accomplishes the following:

1) It alerts his patients to his out-of-town schedule so they may plan accordingly for routine examinations, annual check-ups or preventive care prior to a vacation trip of their own.

2) It explains his absences from the office in a *positive* way rather than leaving to chance, the possibility that his patients will assume he is on holiday or the golf course.

3) It informs his patients that he is keeping up to date and in what fields. Many are surprised at the wide range of services he performs, especially those who have seen him only for "routine matters." It lessens the chance that his patients will go elsewhere if a "specialty need" should arise.

4) It puts his fees in better perspective to those patients who are not aware of the number of hours he devotes to post-graduate study. To the extent that "continuing education" reduces productive office hours, it becomes a factor in setting fees.

5) These courses speak well of his profession and have prompted many inquiries from high school students interested in pursuing it as a career.

The "bulletin board" has worked for this practitioner and many others who have adopted the idea. It may not be your "cup of tea." Before passing it over however, consider this question: In what other way do you communicate these essential facts to your P/Cs?

CONSULTATION ROOM CONSIDERATIONS

Design of new offices is already being influenced by the findings of social scientists on the relationship of space to communications. One new branch of study called proxemics examines how communication between people changes with shifts in the distance between them and the change in position. Even the environment itself is a factor.

For example, many doctors do not use a private office for case presentation or extended discussions with patients, relying instead on the room used for examination or treatment. Their feeling is that it saves time and space, and through the years has become comfortable for them.

It would of course be expected that doctors are comfortable and at-home in the diagnostic areas of their office. They are after all used to the surroundings. But since case presentation is a two-way street, the question becomes: Are their patients at ease under these conditions?

Most of those I've talked with say "no." Seated in an examination chair or perched on the end of an examination table, surrounded by diagnostic equipment, is not a natural situation. It is not conducive to communication.

If, at the same time, the practitioner *stands* while making his recommendations the effect, to the patient, can be felt as "talking down"—literally and psychologically. To the sensitive patient, it is belittling. Even worse, it may give the impression that the practitioner is "hurrying through" to make way for the next patient.

If the patient is also partially disrobed during the discussions, it certainly adds to the patient's mental discomfort and uneasiness. Even the dental patient without his denture or the podiatric patient without her shoes and stockings is understandably self-conscious—notwithstanding the doctor's "professional air" and lack of concern. Such embarrassment, whether justified or not, obviously hinders communication.

It may save a few minutes of time, but it's bad timing to proceed with discussions until the patient has redressed and regained composure.

Adjourning to a sound-proof, private office offers these further advantages:

1) Puts the patient on "home ground" in familiar suroundings that are more comfortable—physically and psychologically.

2) Allows discussions of delicate, intimate or confidential matters to proceed without the patient's fear of being overheard by passers-by or assistants.

3) Compliments the patient by evidencing your added attention and concern. It is but one example of showing more interest than the patient expects or received from the last practitioner.

4) Adds extra importance to your recommendations by making the discussions less casual and hurried.

Are these dividends worth the investment of extra time and space?

Yes, if you are striving to re-orient your practice in a quality direction.

Yes, if current levels of P/C acceptance indicate a need for improvement.

If you don't, at the moment, have a private office to which the patient can be transferred, try setting up a desk in the corner of the examining room. Even a small one is enough to change the setting. Many practitioners have reported a decided improvement in P/C acceptance with this slight variation.

The seating arrangement can also have a bearing on case presentation.

For example, the authoritarian arrangement created by the large "executive desk" with its high back, leather, swivel chair on one side and conventional, smaller chair on the opposite side puts the P/C in a position of "lower rank." To many P/Cs, it creates a feeling that is psychologically degrading and inhibiting.

The new humanized dimension in the business world as well as professional practice is one of down-to-earth, more natural, less assuming postures with people.

As an alternative, place another conventional armchair alongside the one ordinarily reserved for the P/C. Then sit alongside the P/C in this "equal" chair, ignoring the executive chair completely. Your actions suggest: "That's for other people. You're special. Let's talk, friend to friend."

Practitioners who have made this simple change in seating arrangement have told me it makes a world of difference. The P/C is more comfortable, more communicative. Rapport is established more quickly. Case presentations are more easily made, better received.

Note: There may be times when an air of formality and authority is preferable for P/C discussions. The seating arrangement can easily be altered for these situations.

In the design of new offices, many practitioners are using round coffee tables and comfortable captain's chairs for these conferences. Even coffee service is provided to lend informality to the proceedings.

Do any of these variations suggest an idea for "change?"

THE BEGINNINGS OF CHANGE

In effect, I have not given you new ideas, but only new perspectives which serve as signposts to the land of ideas.

Now you must do the rest. You must realize that happiness can be a pink telephone or a kind word.

You must realize that there are new vistas in your relationships with P/Cs.

You must feel the urge to seek these new horizons.

You must put one foot forward and begin the trip.

Actually, it takes so little to make a practice come alive that I am constantly confounded by the inertia that resists a start.

Fortunately, once the start is made, momentum replaces inertia. The dividends are so immediate that the movement to change accelerates as professional life takes on new dimensions.

It leads to greater opportunities to provide more complete and meaningful professional services; it leads to acceleration of referrals; it leads to increased income; it leads to more time for personal pursuits; and it leads to greater enthusiasm for day-to-day practice.

Maurice Chevalier recently celebrated his 80th birthday and was asked: "How does it feel to be 80?" The famous entertainer's reply was: "Considering the alternative, I like it."

The alternative to a humanized, up-to-date, ICA practice is the equivalent of a cold, out-of-date, humdrum practice—for P/Cs, for staff, and for the practitioner.

6

Eight Magic Steps
to Humanize Your Practice
and Accelerate Growth—

Including Sixty-Five
Tested "People Pleasers"

This is a chapter of pure magic.

It is magic that makes your P/Cs aware of and more enthusiastic about an above-average service.

It is magic that nourishes the growth and development of any practice.

I call it magic because these seems to be little of what you can call a cause-effect relationship. A woman's reaction to a vase of flowers in a reception room would seem to have little to do with a referral the client makes soon after. An obstetrician's allowing the pregnant wife and her husband to listen to the fetal heartbeats of their child through the lengthened tubing of his stethoscope would also seem to be little reason for an enthusiastic referral, when viewed in the light of the total birth event.

But surveys of successful practices show such an abundance of the human-touch evidence, that it is impossible for an observer to deny the existence of a very basic cause-effect relationship: The more you give, the more you get.

It is magic—but it isn't a trick, for anyone can do it. You give of yourself to others in little ways—ways that require fractional amounts of time, effort and money. Yet they produce oceans of appreciation and recognition.

Schematically, it looks like this:

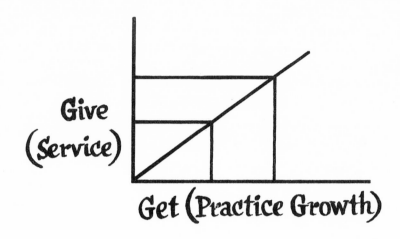

THE HUMAN EQUATION

A recent ad by a prominent airline offered "flub-stubs" worth a dollar if ever their employees failed to come through on a list of eight promises: a friendly greeting, tickets waiting when promised, a smiling stewardess when you board, a special dietary meal when pre-ordered, the best cup of coffee in the sky, frequent announcements from the pilot, a clean plane, a sincere thank you.

There was not one word about getting the passenger to the destination quickly, smoothly, or safely. Why?

The reason is: The passenger assumes it. The primary function, carried out safely and efficiently, is taken for granted.

There are some parallels in professional practice. P/Cs also assume that they will receive a technically competent service. When it is rendered, they leave. No trumpets blare. No special show of gratitude or enthusiasm. No referrals. They received only what they had a right to receive. They got only what they expected and paid for.

In the case of airlines, they use largely the same equipment, their pilots are equally trained and experienced, and they operate to meet the same federal standards and requirements. The only area left in which they can appeal to passengers, on a basis they will understand and appreciate, is in the *personal* realm. The most successful airlines have recognized the importance of the *human equation*. As a result, they have used creative ingenuity to provide liberal amounts of the "human touch."

To the practitioner who is technically competent to the point of brilliance, whose analytical skills and power of penetration border on genius, the message is clear. The *human equation* is an essential fact of practice life.

Walt Disney knew the *human equation* backward and forward.

In Anaheim, California is Walt Disney's "Magic Kingdom," a fabulous playground—something of a fair, a city from the Arabian Nights, a metropolis of the future. It's the most happily inspired, most pleasure-giving park ever conceived. And the most successful.

The park has been called "a land where kings are commoners and commoners are kings." Although dignitaries from the world over, including kings and queens, have visited the park, the fundamental reason for the king-commoner analogy is found in the basic approach to entertaining its visitors.

The training manual for employees, appropriately entitled "You're on Stage at Disneyland," establishes a number of bywords:

"We love to entertain kings and queens, but the vital thing to remember is that every guest receives the VIP treatment."

"It's not just important to be friendly and courteous to the public, it's essential. . . ."

"*Customer* is a bad word. We are hosts and hostesses, and *everyone* who enters our main gate is a guest!"

I could not think of better advice for the "care and handling of P/Cs" in a professional office.

It strikes me as a paradox that some practitioners and their staffs are so cool, abrupt and impersonal on a professional basis, yet *socially* will act very differently.

On an evening at home, for example, while entertaining *friends,* these professional people are the perfect hosts and hostesses—warm, hospitable and friendly.

Why should things be any different the next day for P/Cs who visit the office? Are they not, in a sense, the practitioner's *best friends* who are, in the final analysis, the *paying guests* who make everything possible—professionally *and* personally?

Why not give "airline" service to P/Cs?

Why not think of P/Cs as "guests" in your office "home?"

It's only a difference of perspective, but what a difference it can make in practice growth.

The fact that P/Cs are hungry for personal attention should make practitioners sit up and take notice. But the fact is, most practitioners react just the opposite. They retreat even further behind the barricades of professionalism and up the spiral staircase of the Ivory Tower. They do so in the name of time or for nameless reasons that could be tagged fear or inertia.

How I wish you could see the magical effect that fifteen seconds produced when an Arizona practitioner used a hand puppet to communicate to a frightened child!

THE MAGIC OF HOSPITALITY

Hospitality knows no limits. Catering to a P/C's comfort and peace of mind needs no standard operating limits. It is a personal thing; and, as long as it is sincerely felt by the practitioner and his staff, that feeling will be projected. The "I care" will come through.

The receptionist will be the one with whom the P/C first makes contact. Besides the usual courtesies, here are three field-tested ideas that *any* person, arriving on time for an appointment, would appreciate.

1) Thank the P/C for being prompt. Most people have to rush to keep appointments. It's nice to be appreciated.

2) If there is going to be a delay, explain *why* and *how long* it will be. The explanation might simply be: "I wish everyone was as prompt as you. They have been arriving late all day." This makes sense. It's usually the case. It compliments the P/C *and* places the "blame" where it really belongs.

The alternative is that the P/C may think the practitioner is either badly organized or has "over-booked."

Airline pilots recognize the possibility of this interpretation when they announce: "There are seven planes ahead of us for take-off. Please forgive the delay. We should be cleared in about ten minutes." For longer delays, it is not unsual to have the "no smoking" sign turned off and beverages served, which leads to the next suggestion:

3) Many offices have coffee, tea, or soft-drinks available for waiting P/Cs.

As popular as coffee is, receptionists tell me that most people turn it down; but, of course, all appreciate the gesture and seem to wait a little more patiently, knowing that the practitioner is doing his best and is concerned over the delay.

And that is precisely the point of it all. It's not the coffee, as such. It's the *gesture* of offering it and what it says, loud and clear—"We care."

The alternative to "hospitality" can create negative effects, especially if there is an unreasonable delay. The P/C is just sitting there, annoyed, aggravated, and perhaps running late on her own schedule. There's always the chance of her doing a slow burn, building up resentment, and thinking such thoughts as, "Just who does he think he is?" As a French proverb says: "People count up the faults of those who keep them waiting."

When the P/C is finally ushered in, she is hardly in a receptive or agreeable frame of mind to communicate, listen, or cooperate. The practitioner at this point must be all the more prepared to give her the time and attention to get acclimated and calmed down.

THE MAGIC OF ATTENTION

People are hungry for attention. They want others to be concerned with them, often above and beyond the call of duty. If "things weren't wrong," they might feel differently. If "things weren't wrong," they wouldn't be in your office in the first place.

Hunger for personal attention can be fed in many ways. Many P/Cs go to a professional, ostensibly for advice, when all they really want is an audience. The psychologists call it "verbal ventilation"—a chance to talk things out.

It's all part of the "human equation." You can't fight it, so you might as well know how to become a better listener. It makes people more receptive, friendly and increases the chances for P/C acceptance. Here are five pointers:

1) Listen with your eyes as well as your ears. It shows you are genuinely interested. G.K. Chesterton said, "There is no such thing as an uninteresting subject; there are only uninterested people."

2) Take notes, if appropriate, including a few personal items relating to hobbies or interests. These will come in handy prior to the *next* visit, when a quick glance will provide you with all the clues you need to "break the ice" and make easy conversation, even with a P/C you haven't seen in years. The more insignificant the detail, the better, for it will give you a reputation for a remarkable memory and inform the P/C of your genuine interest and concern. (There is nothing phony about this lubricant to communication since, indeed, you *are* making a special, extra effort to remember these details.)

3) Draw the P/C out. Make the other person feel that what he or she is saying is significant. It is at this point that your "attitude" shows—verbally or non-verbally. Sitting back with your arms folded, for example, has a tendency to *suggest* (depending on your facial expression) an air of "condescension" and "polite indulgence."

4) Listen with your mind. There is a chance for a significant discovery. For example, a veterinarian, discovering there are no children in the family with a pet, can fairly assume that the pet in this case is really the "child," an emotional attachment requiring special handling and care. There are countless examples of "hidden meanings" in the things people say, or don't say. Much can be learned by the inquiring ear.

5) Get involved while listening. Don't be a deadpan. Lean forward. Make a sound every so often. Let the P/C know you are listening.

How do you think the patient felt who was free-associating on the couch when the psychiatrist began to snore? Years later, the story is still making the rounds in that community.

What about the time aspect of attention? It really is not a matter of time. It is more a matter of the attitude behind the listening. Someone can spend twenty minutes with you and you will still feel rushed, while someone else will spend only ten minutes and you will feel satisfied.

THE MAGIC OF PRAISE

Lincoln once began a letter by saying: "Everybody likes a compliment." Psychologist William James said: "The deepest principle in human nature is the craving to be appreciated." He didn't say "wish" or "desire" or even "longing" to be appreciated. He said *"craving"* to be appreciated.

Finding something nice to say about others may seem trivial compared to the value of your professional service, but it satisfies a roaring hunger. It brightens the day, makes them stand a little taller, makes their work-load lighter.

Its value in business was shown in a nationwide poll conducted by the National Retail Dry Goods Association. Thousands of workers and their employers were asked to list, in order of importance, the factors that they felt were of most importance to workers. "Credit for work" was the item that the workers themselves overwhelmingly rated number one. The employers rated this item seventh.

None of us are immune to the value of praise and even the most successful practice would at times be a "hollow nut" were it not for the gratitude and appreciation of P/Cs. And praise begets praise. People will love you for saying kind things and you will feel good for having said them. This is basic human relations, but so often neglected—needlessly.

Here are some praiseworthy tips:

1) Praise P/Cs for their willpower, diligence and persistence, and they'll try even harder.
2) Thank P/Cs for their promptness for appointments and taking care of bills. It has "reinforcement" value.
3) Tell a youngster, "I wish all my patients were as brave as you," and he'll never let you down.
4) Compliment an elderly woman on her hair or an article of clothing. Did you ever notice that some elderly P/Cs get dressed up for their appointments? Don't let them down by ignoring the magic of praise.
5) Transfer praise-received back to P/Cs with "I wish I had a hundred like you."
6) Praise your staff for their efforts, loyalty, and dedication. Thank them for their pleasantness, patience and Potlatch. Practice-building and people-building go hand in hand.
7) Thank your colleagues for their advice, counsel, comradeship, and for the opportunity of associating with them.

Some guidelines for giving praise are:

1) Praise is not praise when it is idle flattery. A lack of sincerity is transparent and can harm. The harassed, hyper-busy, volume-oriented practitioner trying to be a people-oriented and concerned human being is seldom convincing.
2) Praise the *act*, not the person. It doubles the impact, reinforces the sincerity, and creates an incentive for more of the same.
3) Thank people when they least expect it. The "more than expected" aspect of it is what makes it so potent.

THE MAGIC OF CONSIDERATION

On a recent trip to the Soviet Union, many of the groups with whom I met expressed a disenchantment with their country's medical profession. They charged Soviet doctors with being coldhearted and devoid of compassion for patients. They lacked a bedside manner and the right sympathetic words to give patients courage and hope. Several called Soviet doctors inconsiderate.

It's a small world!

Consideration is a magic practice-builder because so few people practice it. It's a busy world!

What is consideration? To Webster, it is thoughtful, sympathetic regard or respect for others.

To P/Cs, it's a plastic, give-away raincoat when they get caught in the office during a sudden rainshower.

It's a phone call on the day of the appointment to advise that, because of an "emergency" or unavoidable delay in the office, the P/C should arrive thirty minutes later or reschedule her appointment, whichever is more convenient.

It's a comfortable office, air-conditioned, with soft music playing.

It's recipes that go well on a new diet or with new dentures.

It's an automobile sticker for out-of-town P/Cs that allows them "free parking" at any of the city's parking meters for the day. These are issued by many city Chambers of Commerce (Fargo, North Dakota and Green Bay, Wisconsin, to name two) for the purpose of encouraging out-of-towners to stay and shop in town.

Obviously, it is impossible to write standard specifications for acts of consideration. It takes concern, imagination, and above all the perspective that recognizes a P/C's *total* needs.

How do commercial firms show consideration? Avis Rent-A-Car has an electric shoe-polishing machine in every station for the convenience of its customers. Hotels are being built to enable guests to park on the floor on which they are staying. Cross-country bus drivers often carry a sewing kit, spot remover, and aspirin for the passenger in need.

A Canadian practitioner keeps a set of jumper battery cables in his office, for people whose cars won't start when they leave in cold weather. Although it was only used twice last season, needless to say, these two people became mighty grateful.

Many non-medical practitioners keep a small oxygen tank in their offices for "emergencies." It only has to be used once to be worth its weight in gold. This is a product commonly available, at minimal cost.

In these days of mini-skirts, thoughtful dentists and podiatrists drape a large towel over their lady patient's lap and legs. It puts the patient at ease.

Most small animal hospitals use newspaper on the floors of animal compartments. A Michigan practitioner, however, uses soft, cotton blankets that are easily washed. Owners *and* pets appreciate this extra consideration.

The telephone offers many ways to be considerate, *or* inconsiderate. Have the telephone company determine the frequency of "busy signals" on your phones. Additional equipment may be needed. Next to a constant busy signal, a "no answer" can be most frustrating. Of course, many practitioners have answering services, but for those who don't, there is automatic answering equipment available. It answers on the first ring, gives the caller a message (in your own voice, if you wish), and records the incoming message.

Real estate brokers use the phone to advise homeowners they are on their way over with a customer. It avoids taking them by surprise. Some even call back after the visit to let them know of the buyer's reaction or decision.

A P/C waiting for news or a report from you may be doing some unnecessary fingernail biting. A call from you can be very welcome and a mind-easer for the family.

For doctors, how about a phone call to the patient the day after office surgery, saying: "I'm just between appointments and was thinking of you. How are you getting along?"

You have made it clear you are busy, so you will not be kept long. If anything is wrong, certainly you want to know. Ironically, some patients are so considerate, they won't bother the doctor unless it's life and death, yet a few simple instructions could ease their pain and worry.

Following hospital surgery, a phone call to the family (even by an aide) will be greatly appreciated. Interestingly enough, many veterinarians do this.

Even more interesting, if not ironic, is the fact that P/Cs tend to remember and talk about these extra kindnesses longer than they do the professional service itself. Chalk it up to human nature.

THE MAGIC OF CONCESSION

"Yes, but. . . ." There is magic in "agreeing quickly" with P/Cs. A polarized negative situation can be built up over nothing, as most practitioners well know.

You can literally "engineer" the consent of dissenting P/Cs by demonstrating that you understand their point of view. You agree with them as far as they go.

Then comes the "but." At that time you can elaborate. They are more receptive because you recognize their point of view. They are more likely to be convinced, easily and effectively.

Few propositions are iron-clad and free from sound, sensible objections—even this one. But, considering the human equation, it pays to be broadminded rather than bull-headed. A Kansas practitioner prints these words as part of his office policy: "We will make every effort to avoid a misunderstanding, to rectify an injustice, or to preserve a friendship."

Concede on little points to demonstrate your flexibility. Then stand firm where it counts.

Sometimes friction develops over fees and collections. It does not pay to make an enemy over a few dollars, despite the "principle of the thing."

Concede. And, if you feel strongly about it, just mark the record card "cash only" for future visits.

A simple overdue amount of $10 can really "bug" some practitioners. First, they write the usual reminder; then comes the familiar succession of stronger and stronger collection letters. Finally, there is the threat of legal action or a lawsuit is started.

Why? If you win, you lose. An enemy in the otherwise friendly camp can hurt.

The whole distasteful cycle is avoided by many practitioners quite simply. The receptionist telephones the P/C to make sure there is no misunderstanding or if there is a logical explanation for the delay. ("We've been away for three months; I'll have a check in today's mail." Or that embarrassing tragedy, "My husband was killed in a car accident last month and I've let everything go; please forgive the delay.")

Sometimes the reply is "I thought $7 covered everything. I see you've added another $3 charge." Whose fault is the misunderstanding? It could be the P/C's for not listening, yours for not explaining clearly, or nobody's. But at least the phone call clears up the situation more satisfactorily than a one-way correspondence or a collection suit.

A California practitioner takes these long overdue small amounts after the usual written and telephone reminders and just "writes them off" at the end of the year. Actually, it amounts to only a small percentage of his gross. Then his receptionist sends a New Year's greeting card with a copy of the bill marked, "Paid in Full—Happy New Year."

Can you guess what happens? Checks begin to arrive, some for the full amount. Some call and, as in the previous example, say they don't feel they owe the $3.00, but are remitting the $7. A "concession" has paid off!

Of course, still others do nothing. But it is still a better path to practice growth, peace of mind and a better community image than bringing suit. Will you concede that?

Getting into frequent quarrels with people and feeling obstinate and defiant is tiring and tension-producing for all concerned. It takes its toll on the practitioner, his staff, his family, and his "innocent" P/Cs who are the indirect recipients of his moods and petty annoyances.

Dr. Walter C. Alvarez, Mayo Clinic consultant emeritus in medicine and nationally read newspaper columnist, writing recently in the professional journal *Modern Medicine* said: "Perhaps one reason why in my early 80s I am still well and active and haven't an ulcer, is that in my daily work I have always avoided conflicts; I love people, and I am particularly fond of eccentric characters (whom some people fight with), and so it is perfectly easy for me to be friends with them. A few of my brilliant friends in medicine could never get or keep a practice, because they were too easily annoyed by patients; too arrogant; too impressed with their own medical dignity; and too inclined to argue violently."

Talk about concession. The July 13, 1968 issue of *Business Week* ran an item about the Indianer Society, a New York City fraternal order of physicians. To gain admission, candidates must make a speech about a patient who doggedly survived despite their worst mistakes in judgment.

Concession with a capital "C".

THE PRACTICE-BUILDING MAGIC OF ASSURANCE

The P/C is usually in a jungle of uncertainty. His problem has taken him out of his element and set him down in strange surroundings. He is uncertain about what will happen next and anxious about the outcome.

He needs assurance.

I agree that because of legal, technical, ethical or other reasons, it is not always possible to guarantee the future, or even explain with certainty the past. You cannot make promises that are not within your power to keep. It is better to be prudent and conservative rather than overly optimistic, to be safe rather than "out on a limb" from which there is no retreat.

I have heard statements such as "Nothing in life is certain except death and taxes,"

"I don't have a crystal ball," "It depends on too many things." Such statements, no matter how true, can compound the P/C's fears and his fertile imagination can aggravate symptoms and problems, physically and psychologically. His outlook becomes confused, causing him alarm and a premature sense of defeat. In short, he panics.

Psychologists tell us that such negative reactions can militate against recovery or cause further deterioration. They point out that witnesses in court or at income tax reviews often experience a shattering of composure that renders their testimony totally ineffective.

We vote for a compromise.

Whenever possible, at least an inkling of assurance should be offered. Of course, it should be based on conditions and events. But at least it should provide something to go on, or hang onto, or a goal to work toward.

Assurance, no matter how tenuous, can keep P/C spirits up, incentive going, and enthusiasm in high gear.

We have been talking basically about survival assurance, matters of life and death, of guilty or not guilty, that may have no basis in fact, but nevertheless lurk in the P/C mind.

There are several other kinds of assurance:
—Reassurance
—Encouragement
—Inspiration

Reassurance is mild. It allays P/C fears and anxieties. It says, in effect, "Don't worry." It does not say what you should do in place of worry. In fact, it smacks of patronizing to the P/C, as if you were just telling her something because she wanted to hear it.

Reassurance, with an added explanation, is stronger. Again, the airlines have recognized this principle when making the routine announcement during landing procedures: "The noise you hear is the normal sound of the landing gear being lowered and locked into position" which casually explains the strange, rumbling sounds of jets that can frighten passengers.

Many health-care practitioners give patients a "no need for concern" list. It is a *printed* reassurance, spelling out events, symptoms or reactions following treatment which, although unexpected, may occur. Some add "what to do" if pain, swelling, discharge, dizziness, etc., do occur.

Encouragement is stronger. It is reassurance fortified by facts, amplified by details, and reinforced by a pat on the shoulder or a firm handshake. If reassurance can be symbolized by "don't worry," then encouragement can be symbolized by "everything is going to be all right."

Inspiration is assurance in its highest and most effective form. Inspiration literally means "breathing in" and you can breathe into your P/Cs such priceless gifts as hope, courage, and power.

When people are in a high state of expectation and belief, your words have the same effect as suggestions to a hypnotized subject. You can crush them with gloom and doom or raise them to ten feet tall with hope, optimism, and confidence. They then live out your words. "I have every confidence in you, Mrs. Smith."

Assurance, in its many forms, pays off in P/Cs' peace of mind. Without that peace of mind, they will not rest. They will call you, often in the middle of the night, to double check on what you said, searching for that assurance which will allow them that peace of mind.

Assurance is a practice-builder. However, like anything else, it needs to be used in moderation.

Do not over-sell. If you hint at the positive outcome, it is much more effective than painting it in vivid colors. Overstate and you are blamed when there are only 75 percent results. Understate and, when things work out better than expected, the P/C is truly enthusiastic.

THE MAGIC OF GOOD NATURE AND A SENSE OF HUMOR

Good nature is also part of the "human equation." It strips us of our occupational armor and permits the person to shine through. Good nature is human nature and the force it exerts for P/C acceptance and practice growth would surprise many.

Good nature is inside us all, but we inhibit ourselves. Professionals are often the most inhibited. Chalk it up to their "stature."

The politician, striving for stature, never fails to shake a hand, cast a wink, or flash a smile. He knows that, although the skyscraper reaches for the sky, it must also begin at the grass roots to be believed.

Gelett Burgess, the famous humorist, tells of how he once was so uplifted by laughter, that he filled a scrapbook with all the laughing pictures he could find in newspapers and magazines. Then he loaned it to a hospital.

The nurse who saw it roared. The book was passed from patient to patient, bed to bed, ward to ward. Guffaws filled the corridor. Many smiled for the first time in months. The doctors testified that this laugh-cure almost always produced a marked improvement.

Laughter is real medicine. It's a breath of fresh air in a morose world. It warms up the world. It is therapy in its own right.

Used as French chefs use garlic—discretely and sparingly—a little humor in the professional office can ease tensions and, at times, be an ideal supplement to practice routine.

Dr. Leonard Hymes, Professor at the Pennsylvania College of Podiatric Medicine, maintains a private practice in Pleasantville, New Jersey. His pleasing ways are no mere coincidence. He "kids" with older patients, discussing things in a youthful manner with them. He'll ask if they have done too much dancing lately or if they hurt their foot when they fell off the bar stool. He says they like this good-natured ribbing even though they know he is not being serious. They enjoy the repartee and the reminder that they might be a younger person than they think they are.

The practitioner that "seasons" his service with a dash of the "light touch" is at ease with himself and his P/Cs. He projects an aura of confidence and success and, like all positive emotions, it is contagious.

A dentist I know whistles and hums as he works. It's really quite disarming to the patients who are braced and taut with fear of the unknown. The fact that he whistles terribly and hums off key interferes not one iota with the complete change of emotional polarity he is able to effect. It possibly helps.

The Greek historian Herodotus tells us of an ancient king of Egypt, one Amasis, who used to work hard half the day and then relax and swap jokes the other half. To critical counselors, he explained his habits by saying that, if the archer did not unstring his bow after the battle, it would lose its snap and it would be no good to him when he needed it again.

Laughter unstrings the "emotional bow," and permits it to keep its elasticity. That is why men have liked jokes ever since they began to talk, and will go on liking them as long as they continue to be burdened with tensions and anxieties—and that, I suspect, will be a rather long time.

Are we suggesting jokes? Or puns? No. These can be dangerous. Humor is always inappropriate when it is carried to an extreme or used at the P/C's expense. It is ineffective when it is false and put on.

A practitioner in Alabama has a quotation of Josh Billins, framed in his consultation room, which reads: "Laffing iz the sensation of pheeling good all over, and showing it principally in one spot." He told me it serves as a reminder of the value of the "light touch."

Humor also has educational value:

A New York City driving instructor gives his pupils small stickers, for their car's dashboard, that read: "Please Fasten Your Seat Belts—Somebody Loves You."

In Beaverton, Oregon, three pharmacists, using some rather "grim" humor, are marketing a cigarette called "Cancer." Appropriately enough, the pack is funeral-black with the usual admonition, all the more poignant, "Smoking may be hazardous to your health."

An optician in Missouri, grown tired of making explanations and apologies to patients who wanted same-day deliveries of their prescription lenses, had a sign made which he placed on the dispensing table. It read: "Of course I want my glasses today! If I wanted them tomorrow, I would have come in tomorrow." He confesses it doesn't always "work," but it never fails to get a chuckle and an understanding nod.

In these mad-mod times, "buttons" have become a new form of communication on subjects ranging from the sublime to the ridiculous. I've encountered many being distributed by practitioners, some more serious than others. For the most part, they're given to children, but you'd be surprised at the number of grown-ups who also enjoy them:

"Stamp Out Dental Neglect"
"My Doctor Loves Me"
"Member of the 20/20 Vision Club"
"I Have Happy Feet"
"My Teeth Are O.K. Club"
"For Bravery In The Doctor's Office"
"Candy Is Dandy But Sex Won't Rot Your Teeth"

In the parlance of movie censorship, this last one is rated "M". And last but not least, the button that perhaps best summarizes this part of the chapter (rated "G"):

Smile button ideas: A Texas practitioner wrote me of using the "smile button" as a "graduation diploma" to patients completing extended treatment. A Minnesota practitioner varies this idea by pinning a button on an occassional out-going letter to establish a friendly mood or to express sincere appreciation for a favor done. (One important difference between correspondence and conversation is the inability to convey a "smile" in the former—the lack of which may change the entire meaning and tone of a letter.)

THE MAGIC OF POTLATCH

Potlatch is giving more to P/Cs than they expect. When they discover Potlatch in your office, their professional visits lose some of the stigma of a duty they must perform and gain the flavor of voluntary experience.

Potlatch can be the difference between *captive* P/Cs and *captivated* P/Cs. It's but another alternative to inter-personal relations in your practice.

Here are some Potlatch ideas that others are using successfully. My motive—to motivate you.

A practitioner in Pittsburgh, with a large geriatric practice, surprises his elderly women patients when they visit him on or near their birthday with a box of candy. Its uniqueness is enhanced by a greeting card as part of the cover. It reads: "You are nice and . . . nice people deserve nice things . . . I hope you enjoy this gift. . . ." **

When the candy is shared with friends and relatives, you can bet his name is mentioned; yet it would be unfair, knowing this practitioner as I do, to say that his motive is to generate referrals. He genuinely likes his P/Cs, and the gesture of "giving more" is just part of his nature.

Potlatch is never the motive for practice-building as such, but practice growth is the inevitable byproduct. The real motive is to communicate concern for others and to demonstrate the personal touch.

---

* A catalog including the "Smile Button" is available from Spectex Inc., Box 451, Great Neck, New York, 11022.
** Contemporary Candies, made by The Dari-Fresh Co., Melrose Park, Illinois 60160.

Sales Consultant Elmer Wheeler stressed the idea, "Say it with flowers." Actually, there's no nicer, warmer way to express one's thoughts than with nature's bounty. Here are some variations that all say, "I care."

A single flower to visiting women P/Cs on Mother's Day or Valentine's Day.

A Texas practitioner sends his hospitalized women patients a "pillow corsage." An ordinary bouquet would not have the same effect; it would be overdoing it. The "pillow corsage," diminutive and appropriate, qualifies for the "Potlatch award."

An Idaho practitioner has a local florist deliver one red rose and a thank-you note to those women who send him several referrals. This single flower conveys the sentiment without the ostentation and expense of a dozen roses.

A Connecticut practitioner, when sending flowers as condolence to the family of a deceased client, times his gift imaginatively. He sends flowers *after* the funeral, usually on a Sunday, a week or so later. For many, this is the loneliest and saddest time of adjustment.

Dr. Jack Antelyes, a prominent New York veterinarian, on those occasions when a hospitalized pet dies from disease or injuries, sends his clients a condolence note. Each letter is individually written and contains some personal reference to the pet and its family relationship. As he told me, "We recognize and understand *their* loss—truly and sincerely." His clients' loyalty and promptness in paying these bills attest to the effectiveness of his "I Care Attitude."

In the healing art professions, many practitioners give their patients "before" and "after" x-ray (positives) or polaroid pictures of their conditions. Many patients appreciate these "souvenirs" and show them proudly to relatives and friends during the retelling of their "ordeal."

A California pharmacist sends out a "get-well" card to all people for whom he fills a prescription.

A Georgia bank drive-in teller gives a "bone biscuit" to dog "passengers" in the cars that come to his window.

Potlatch can be anywhere—in the reception room in the form of a candy bowl with chocolate kisses, balloons for the little ones (or for grandmother to take to them). It can be a strand of "worry beads" * to "occupy" a nervous P/C. Potlatch can entertain or educate.

How about booklets—on "Safety in the Home," or on the highway, or in sports—which provide practical information and advice? ** Many P/Cs might otherwise never be aware of these precautions in daily living.

The Public Health Service has designed a new and educational game to help the elderly become better acquainted with the health benefits available through Medicare. Called "Medigame," played with a board, cards and dice, it is being distributed to senior citizens' groups and pre-retirees in industry.

A California real-estate broker gives his new homeowners a "Welcome Neighbor"

---

* Called Komboli by the Greeks, worry beads date back hundreds of years. Actually, they have nothing to do with worrying, nor do they have any religious significance, nor are they a cure for anything. Their "power" as a "pacifier" does, however, keep idle hands busy.

** A catalog of safety booklets is available from Channing L. Bete Co., Inc., 45 Federal Street, Greenfield, Mass. 01301.

brochure which includes illustrated facts about the electrical, plumbing and construction materials and how to get the best service from them; a vacation checklist of safety measures while the family is away; the basic steps to a successful lawn; and helpful hints for fire protection.

Some veterinarians give clients, who are planning to take their dogs on vacation with them, a booklet entitled "Touring with Towser." * It is a directory of hotels and motor courts that accommodate guests with dogs. "Travelling Abroad with Your Pet" ** lists the requirements for taking dogs and cats into foreign countries.

The American Institute of Certified Public Accountants has developed a brochure entitled "The Layman's Guide to Preparing Financial Statements for Churches." Thoughtful practitioners make this booklet available to local volunteer church officials.

Instead of the usual greeting card, a Connecticut insurance agent sends his clients an actual full-size reproduction of the front page of *The New York Times,* published on the day they were born. One I saw was dated October 8, 1922, and told of dial phones being used for the first time.†

These examples of Potlatch are designed to show the wide variety of interesting ideas that creative and considerate practitioners in varied fields have used to humanize their practices.

The common thread throughout this chapter is the idea of giving the P/C something "extra," above and beyond the call of duty, not with the expectation of practice growth as such, but for the sheer joy of doing and giving. The "magic" of these efforts is that they have a habit of rebounding. In the long run, the giver is the one who somehow benefits—for, as William Shakespeare wrote, "We are advertised by our loving friends."

---

* "Touring with Towser" available from Gaines Dog Research Center, General Foods Corp., White Plains, N.Y. 10602. Enclose 50¢.

** "Travelling Abroad with Your Pet" available from Education Department, ASPCA, 441 East 92nd Street, New York, New York 10028, 25¢ each.

† Available for $1.65 plus tax, dating back to 1851 from *The New York Times,* Front Pages Department, New York, New York 10036.

7

How to Preach
What You Practice

The Ivory Tower is more than a successful courtroom drama by playwright Jerome Weidman. It is an unsuccessful office attitude that stifles practice growth for many professionals. Webster defines the Ivory Tower, figuratively, as a place of mental withdrawal from reality and action, used as a symbol of escapist tendencies.

From the Ivory Tower, many professionals look down on their P/Cs. But they do not single out P/Cs; they also look down on the community at large. At times, they are detached and insulate themselves from the need for human relations and personal involvement.

If the public "senses" this detachment, the practitioner, as well as his profession at large, suffer from this "image," whether it's real or imagined. And that's where "public relations" comes into the picture.

Notwithstanding the somewhat negative image the term "public relations" has—especially in the professional community—what it really amounts to is "preaching what you practice." It's doing the right thing and then letting people know you are doing it. It's "getting involved" on a person-to-person basis, as well as on a community-wide basis.

Public relations, when used by practitioners for personal gain, is of course taboo. However, when public relations is undertaken for the purpose of educating and motivating the community at large on broader aspects of the profession, the interpretation is different.

For example, the medical profession in the United States has been "thrown" somewhat by the behavior of Dr. Christiaan Barnard, the South African heart transplant surgeon. His frequent television appearances and newspaper interviews appear to some of his American colleagues as publicity-motivated.

Dr. Barnard is unmoved by such criticism, since he feels—centered as it is on a breakthrough in surgery—these newstories are beneficial to medicine in general. He cites total strangers who have made research grants to the profession because of their viewing and reading about heart transplants, not to mention an increasing number of "donors."

Once a practitioner accepts the obligation or willingness to do good—or enlightened self-interest, if you like—then public relations takes on a different perspective. It is, at this point, but another form of "communication" to inform and to enlighten. A better term might be "public service."

The book *Between Parent and Child*,* by Dr. Hiam Ginott, that remained on the best-seller list for about a year, may have won recognition for its author, but it did far more total good for psychologists all over the country by awakening people to the need to bridge the communications gap and to utilize the skills psychologists have to offer. Many popular books by practitioners in the field of law, medicine, accounting, etc., have served their professions well.

Education takes place at many levels, and it is a continuing process. The means are limited by which the public can be educated on the need for total service—medical, legal, fiscal, and in other professional areas. The most important means of all are the practitioners themselves.

THE PROFESSIONAL COMMUNICATIONS GAP

The Ohio Osteopathic Association of Physicians and Surgeons recently conducted a survey in Columbus and Dayton, under the auspices of the College of Administrative Sciences of Ohio State University, concerning the image of the osteopathic physician. The survey revealed that only twenty percent of the public could accurately define a D. O. The result was an association-sponsored program to educate the public in the education and licensing requirements of the osteopathic profession in Ohio.

Many first-time P/Cs have no conception of the background, training, and breadth of services rendered by professional specialists. What little they do know in many cases is out of date and based on limited past experiences or hearsay.

Part of the problem is the information explosion. The emergence of new professions and new areas of specialization brings with it ever-increasing educational requirements and standards of performance. According to the U.S. National Aeronautics and Space Administration, 90 percent of all scientists who ever lived are alive

---

* Dr. Hiam Ginott, *Between Parent and Child* (Macmillan Co., N.Y., 1965).

today. Two-thirds of all the products that we will buy twenty years from now have yet to be developed. Over half of the children in grades 1 through 6 today will be employed in occupations that do not presently exist.

The individual practice growth with which we have been concerned is, of course, only part of the bigger picture of achieving growth and recognition of the profession at large.

Many, if not most, professions are handicapped by the public's limited knowledge of what they actually do. Public Accounting, for example, as a relatively new profession lacks the traditions of law and medicine. It has developed tremendously in the last fifty years, but the public's appreciation of its scope has lagged far behind. Many people take a narrow view of the accountant's ability to serve, thinking of him largely in terms of auditing and taxes or, even more narrowly, as only an expert bookkeeper whose main job is the detection of bookkeeping errors or the verification of facts already known. In this regard, many consider his services as a burdensome expense or "necessary evil."

Yet, today's accountant is a highly trained professional, capable of rendering a broad range of management and tax-related services directly concerned with the production of profits for the businessman and the economic well-being of the individual.

In the architectural profession, as another example, one of the problems is that the average layman still views a building according to its cosmetic interest. He should, of course, evaluate it in terms of how well it serves its social purpose, how efficiently it operates, what it means financially to the owner and the community, whether it represents an improvement over what it replaced, and how well it fits into the neighborhood and the community.

These communications gaps, certainly for the public at large, are beyond the scope and ability of the individual practitioner to do much about. However, on a state, regional and national basis, many professional associations have embarked on a public relations program to inform the public.

ASSOCIATION-SPONSORED PROGRAMS

In 1965, a Gallup poll indicated that only 13 percent of the people interviewed could correctly identify the profession of optometry. Although 80 percent did know that optometrists are concerned with vision, many judged the profession by standards dating back to the days of "jewelry store practices."

In November 1965, as part of the Nebraska Optometric Association's Public Information Program, the following ad was placed in the *Nebraska Newspaper* pointing out the function and importance of the optometrist as a specialist in today's world. The *Nebraska Newspaper* is published monthly by the Nebraska Press Association and goes to all newspaper editors in the state.

The Optometrist—Today's Specialist

Today's optometrist is a specialist in the art and science of visual care. Through training and experience, he combines a knowledge of anatomy, physiology, general and ocular pathology, psychology and optics. He provides the following complete visual service:

1. Taking case history to learn essential facts about the patient.

2. Use of many thorough methods for the detection of eye disease or the symptoms of other diseases as evidenced in the eyes.

3. Referral to a medical practitioner if disease is detected.

4. Refraction of eyes to determine whether they are focusing light rays to best advantage.

5. Vision analysis of far acuity, near acuity, field of vision, depth of perception, ocular coordination, and color perception.

6. Procedures for detection of neuromuscular impairment of binocular function and its correction.

7. Adaptation of conventional or contact lenses to meet the needs of the individual patient.

8. Prescription and fitting of telescopic and microscopic devices for the "near-blind."

9. Use of orthoptics and visual training to re-educate visual skills and improve visual performance.

The optometrist's prime function is to enable each patient to see clearly, efficiently and comfortably. Considerations of eye efficiency and eye comfort keynote important advances in the science of vision care. Visual examinations that analyze all aspects of the seeing process are an outstanding contribution of optometry to human welfare.

—Nebraska Optometric Association

Public relations, in this sense, brings to the public's attention the function and value of a well-trained profession. It creates a more conscious awareness of problems which the profession is equipped to solve. It produces a greater understanding and appreciation of professional training, services and fees. For the individual practitioner, it shortens the length of time it takes people to recognize him for what he does.

Here is another example of this:

The Consulting Engineers Council of Colorado recently ran an eight-page, color-illustrated supplement to the Sunday papers in Denver, entitled: "Consulting Engineering—Progress Through Professional Service." Among the subjects discussed were: code of ethics, how to select an engineer, what is a consulting engineer, when to seek the services of a consultant, careers in consulting engineering.

An example from this supplement that illustrates how this program has aided in keeping their professional image up-to-date, follows:

"His skill may be electrical engineering, hydraulics, highway engineering, sewerage systems, lighting, air conditioning, process engineering, soil mechanics, structural, mechanical, civil or chemical engineering, or any of dozens of other specializations.

"He can give good counsel, from the planning into the operational stage of any project. In particular, because of projects he is working on daily, he has a ready knowledge of costs, sources of supply, the suitability of different types of material, equipment or processes to do the job, and many other factors affecting the planning and realization of a project.

"He is equally ready to apply these and other elements of his knowledge and skill —in making preliminary analyses and reports, estimating budgets, preparing project designs, supervising construction or operations, providing liaison with architects, suppliers, contractors and regulatory agencies, and offering technical counsel in litigation. He knows when other specialists are needed, whom to select and how to supervise their work."

The obvious benefits of such association-sponsored programs make it one of the many reasons that practitioners in all professions should join their state and national associations. Their dues, collectively pooled, can do much to further their profession's public image and enhance the quality and quantity of service rendered to the public at large.

INFORM THOSE WHO INFORM THE PUBLIC

Magazines, newspapers, radio and TV can be "cost-free" vehicles for informing the public. Their editors and program directors are constantly looking for story ideas and timely subjects. The advances being made in professional technologies more than qualify for those news stories but, like the P/C, these people will not beat a path to your profession's door for something they don't know about.

A story that has "news value"—geared to their audience's needs and interests—will find them most receptive and eager to listen.

The March 1969 issue of *Redbook*, for example, included a feature article entitled: "The Return of the Midwife," written by Beth Day.* It pointed out that the modern midwife, now considered a respectable member of the obstetrical fraternity, is a far cry from the "granny" of yesteryear who called for boiling water and torn sheets. According to standards established by the American College of Nurse Midwifery, today's midwife is a "registered professional nurse who has successfully completed a recognized program, ranging from eight months for a certificate in nurse-midwifery to two years for a master's degree in public health."

Such articles take on an importance that transcends the obvious "publicity value" for this profession. To quote further from the article: "In this country more babies are born every year than there are doctors available to deliver them. . . ." What makes the situation even more critical is "that much of this nation's shocking infant-mortality rate (the United States ranks 13th in the world) is attributed to lack of adequate prenatal care."

The value, in this case, of "informing the public," especially in remote areas of the country, takes on a limitless importance. It becomes "public service" of the highest order.

THE ONE PUBLIC SERVICE ACTIVITY
THAT MOST CONTRIBUTES TO PRACTICE GROWTH

Professionals who regularly appear on the speaker's platform tend to have more successful practices than those who do not. Therefore, it is logical to expect a planned

---

* Beth Day, "The Return of the Midwife," *Redbook,* March, 1969. Copyrighted © 1969 by McCall Corporation.

program of public speaking to aid practice growth as well as to enhance the standing of your profession in the community.

Are these motives selfish? Possibly. However, I report it here as a fact of life, not as an approved motive. I agree that your motives are important and that the practitioner who seeks only to attract new P/Cs probably won't make as good a speech or as good an impression on the community as the practitioner whose primary motive is to share his ideas with his fellow man, and thus better serve his community. On the other hand, there is nothing wrong in wanting a successful practice which incorporates rendering more complete and extensive services. Speaking in public is but one additional way the practitioner can expand his service and increase his value to the community.

Many non-speaking practitioners are sensitive and concerned that they will be considered "too pushy" or "commercial" or "unethical" in seeking and accepting public speaking engagements. The community, however, views it differently and has the opposite reaction. Local citizens are much more likely to regard these practitioners as "civic minded," "interested in service," or other worthwhile motive, rather than practice-building as such.

Professionals frequently express surprise that local groups would care to hear them speak. A different perspective was expressed, for example, in a recent news item reported in the *Michigan MVMA Newsletter:*

> A demand for veterinarians to give demonstrations, present action exhibits and conduct tours for civic groups was voiced by the first Michigan 4-H Veterinary Science Workshop sponsored by the MVMA, AVMA, and the National 4-H Service Committee. Over 165 adults and junior leaders agreed such action would give the public a clearer understanding of veterinary medicine, related careers and their personal health.

This study in Michigan helps point up the fact that health care, including veterinary science, is not only the third largest industry in the U.S.A., but is also one of the least understood.

The public needs to know more about the services of all professions and the advantages of preventive maintenance. They need to know the ABCs of professional care.

I am not going to bore you with statistics. They prove only a small percentage of our population is seeking complete professional service. You name your profession and there is overwhelming evidence to prove that your colleagues could double their practice overnight with a proper saturation program of public education.

Thus, it is not difficult to make a case that practitioners have an *obligation* to speak about their profession as well as an *opportunity* to upgrade their image and accelerate practice growth.

Professional associations are well aware of this. They are constantly planning educational activities. Their speakers' bureaus need members' assistance. Here is one outlet for the practitioner interested in expanding his communications beyond his P/C circle to benefit the entire profession.

Keep the purpose clearly in mind lest the motivation be blurred. Public speaking is aimed at widening the horizons of public understanding about the benefits of full professional services. Your own practice is scrupulously bypassed—no reference to it whatsoever. Use examples and case studies from other practices or research projects. Avoid any cause for misinterpretation. Attempt to share the event with colleagues.

HOW TO GET RECOGNIZED AS AN AUTHORITY

The average practitioner has all of the qualifications and the ability he needs to become an effective public speaker. It is simply an extension of in-office P/C education.

Professional people do not first become regarded as an expert, then speak in public. More often, they begin to speak in public, then find themselves classed as an expert (both inside and outside their profession). Surveys show that once a professional begins to speak in public, he is more highly regarded in every respect, including his professional skills and knowledge. Rightly or wrongly, most people seem to reason: "He must be an authority, or he wouldn't be speaking on the subject."

Incidentally, I have found that many professional people, because of real or imagined modesty, tend to downgrade themselves as public speakers. But the fact is, just how much of an authority do you have to be to talk about your profession, whether it's to an individual or to a group? It's really the same thing on a larger scale.

HOW TO DEVELOP
A DYNAMIC PLATFORM PERSONALITY

Don't try. The demand today is not for orators to give flowery speeches but for speakers to give informative talks. And, while there is such a thing as a dynamic platform personality, trying to develop one directly as an end itself is self-defeating. The pseudo-dynamic personality misses his target and comes across as superficial and phony.

Be yourself. That's good enough. Don't copy anyone else. Concentrate on the message you want to get across and you may, like Winston Churchill, end up being a personality.

Churchill was one of the most dynamic speakers of this century. Yet he once said that he never attempted to become a good speaker as an end in itself, but that he had certain ideas he wanted to express and he constantly strove to express them as well as he could. At the onset, he had a speech impediment. He never completely overcame it, but his "slurry" way of running words together became a dynamic, distinguishing personality trait for him.

HOW TO GET RID OF STAGE FRIGHT

Don't try to get rid of it. Use it. This is the secret of the pros.

Understanding just what the butterflies are can help tremendously. They are not a sign of personal inferiority. They are not proof positive that you are not the type to speak in public. And, depending on how you yourself handle them, they do not even necessarily mean that you're afraid or anxious.

Actually, the butterflies are a sign of strength rather than weakness. All good speakers have them and, in fact, worry when they don't. Even an accomplished platform personality such as Dr. Billy Graham—"Mr. Poise" himself—said in a recent newspaper column that he had never made a talk in public that he did not feel butterflies at the outset.

Psychologists tell us that at the outset, and in their pure form, what we call butterflies are not fear or anxiety or another emotion, but simple emotional excitement. Thus, excitement is basically a reinforcement—hence, a *power* rather than a weakness. It can reinforce whatever tendency we may decide upon. If we intend to run away or if our thoughts are taken up with escape, then this excitement can reinforce our ability to run faster by making us afraid.

But, if we intend to go forward rather than run away, and if we keep our thoughts mainly on the positive goal of making a speech rather than wishing we could get out of it, then we will find this same emotional excitement acts as a shot in the arm, reinforcing our ability to think clearly and speak better. It puts zip into our presentation. And speakers who don't have it come across as dull and drab.

Usually the butterflies are acutely uncomfortable for only about two minutes after you begin to speak. Ignore them—Begin—Go forward! The discomfort will disappear and you'll speak better. The more you do this, the less discomfort you'll feel.

And, if your suffering is too acute, you can always overcome it by joining one of the excellent public speaking classes or schools operating in most cities today. An Albany, New York dentist did this recently and enjoyed it so much he went on to become a volunteer instructor for future classes, thus creating additional opportunities.

HOW TO MOTIVATE AN AUDIENCE

Telling isn't teaching. Listening isn't learning. "Communication," whether it's to an audience or to an individual P/C, is meaningless and ineffective if it fails to *motivate* the listener and produce *positive* action.

You, as a dedicated practitioner, are and should be interested in the technical aspects of your profession. And that's as it should be, for that's the reason you chose your profession in the first place and the love of your work, as such, helps make you a competent practitioner. Because of this fact, you may prefer to talk about your profession and its work, as an end in itself.

But keep in mind your audiences do not have your background and orientation and do not share your personal interest in the technical procedures, aspects and equipment related to your services. Thus, what you may like to talk about is not necessarily what your audience will like to hear. Your professional services become interesting to an audience only when they can be seen as a means to some end which already holds their main or supplementary interest.

Your job is to find some already existing interest of your audience and show how your profession can help to fulfill these desires or interests.

Local police groups, for example, provide a ready-made and receptive audience for professional people who can assist them in the line of duty. A talk on "Vision," in this case, would have less value than a talk on "Vision as Related to Highway Safety," or even more specifically a presentation on the subject of "How to determine if a driver is wearing contact lenses, and how to remove them from an unconscious victim."

A Michigan practitioner has helped his community by lecturing to local police and firemen on the subject of "Midwife Training for Rescue Squads," while another in Missouri has lectured extensively throughout the state to law enforcement and civil defense groups on the subject of "Radiation and the Public Safety."

The rule of gearing the talk to the audience's interests also holds true when you're talking before high school groups on Career Days. On these occasions, you will, of course, be expected to present more facts about your profession—what it entails, its scope, what professional practice in the field means to the individual, and what is required. In other words, you'll be expected to present more pure facts about your specialty and its practice. But, to attract young people into the profession, remember that psychologically it is virtually impossible for anyone to develop any interest in anything truly new, unless the "new" in some way ties into some old or existing interest.

Many high school students you'll talk with have little, if any, interest in your specialty, per se. But they *are* interested in personal achievement. Most young people are highly idealistic. They are interested in self-fulfillment, in finding a life's work that will enable them to contribute something worthwhile to their community and to mankind. They're interested in the personal satisfaction that comes from serving others.

Show how your profession can help them achieve these ends and you'll touch a powerful, built-in, pre-existing interest.

HOW TO INCREASE INTRA- AND
INTER-PROFESSIONAL REFERRALS

Professional colleagues, or those in related fields, also provide ready-made, receptive groups with whom you can share ideas of common interest. As an instructor to these groups, you can also preach what you practice—for their benefit as well as yours.

In these times of rapidly changing technologies and ever-increasing specialties, no profession is an "island." Practitioners are becoming more and more dependent on each other for guidance and advice on matters that vitally affect their practice and their P/Cs.

Human needs can no longer be fragmented. We are learning that everything depends on everything else, that causes, effects and solutions often arise as a combination of many factors—social, economic, physical, psychological, and legal, etc.

For example, the "slow-learner" in the classroom may have a vision problem, a psychological block, or a genetic deficiency.

The etiology of drug addiction, divorce, and countless other problems of our society is no longer a simple, clear-cut matter.

To recognize the P/C's total needs, it is essential that practitioners be *aware* of the many influences that shape and determine that P/C's problem. It requires that they *learn* as much as possible from other specialists whose interests and objectives overlap theirs.

At the same time, *teaching* also provides tremendous opportunities to share with others ideas that will aid them in the management of their practice. These may include subjects related to P/C management as well as topics of law, accounting, taxes, investments, insurance, malpractice, etc., related to *office* management.

Many practitioners have found that conducting these courses for inter- and intra-professional groups combines service with the opportunity to establish a base for future *referrals*.

If a member of these audiences is aware of P/C needs (or his own for that matter) beyond his competence to evaluate or serve, it is logical that he would refer to, or seek the advice of, the practitioner who is "best-known" on this subject. Public speaking, therefore, becomes not only an opportunity for "public service" but also a "showcase" for a practitioner's knowledge and ability and ultimately another route to becoming "known" and "recognized" as an authority.

Doctors, lawyers, accountants, engineers, educators, realtors, psychologists, and community planners are among the endless list of those with whom it is possible to share ideas and information of common interest, as a "student" or as an "instructor."

Contacts between individuals and groups are an integral part of our daily personal and professional lives. In this complex world, these contacts and interpersonal relationships have become highly complicated and inter-dependent. Public speaking and public relations are activities available to a practitioner to bring his profession's image up-to-date, to assist the professional community, to better serve the public, and to increase referrals.

TEST YOUR R.Q. (REFERRAL QUOTIENT)

Here is a questionnaire we've used in seminars and which practitioners have found useful as a handy checklist, not only in testing their Referral Quotient but as a reminder from week to week about the care and handling of personal and professional referrals.

1) Do you *routinely* ask new P/Cs: "By whom were you referred?" _____
_____

2) (a) Do you *routinely* acknowledge P/C referrals to your office? _____ If so, is it by phone _____, in person (on your next "chance" meeting) _____, by pre-printed card or letter _____, by personal note _____?
(b) Is it within 48 hours _____, one week _____, one month _____?

3) Do those who send multiple referrals, say a dozen or more, receive any *special* acknowledgement? _____

4) (a) In receiving referrals on a "consulting basis" from professional colleagues,

do you *routinely* report back promptly? _____ If so, is it written _____
____, by telephone _____, both _____?
(b) Do you faithfully return P/Cs to the referring practitioner? _____

5) Do you acknowledge referrals today, now that your practice is well-established, as enthusiastically as you did in the early days of your practice? _____

6) (a) Do you keep "statistics" on the number of in-coming personal and professional referrals to your office? _____
(b) Have these decreased in recent years? _____
(Compare the answers to this question with those of numbers 2, 3, 4, and 5.)

7) As a patient, client, or customer yourself, do you have occasion to make referrals to business and professional people in your community? _____

8) (a) As a patient, client or customer yourself, do you appreciate a word of "thanks" from the office (firm) to whom your referrals are sent? _____
(b) Would a written note have more impact and remembrance value? _____
(Compare the answers to this question with those of number 2.)

9) (a) Does a colleague's response to your sending *him* a referral, in any way affect your future referrals to him? _____
(b) Does an obvious lack of appreciation, a failure to say "thank you" and complete indifference leave you with any negative "second thoughts?" _____
(c) Would another colleague, equally competent, but more appreciative, tend to get your future referrals? _____
(Compare the answers to this question with those of numbers 2 and 4.)

10) (a) In an established "general" practice, what percent of P/Cs would you estimate are derived from referred cases? _____%
(b) Estimate the possible chain reaction effects that might accrue as a result of *one* referral to your office (i.e. the *number* of P/Cs in the *new* P/C's circle of friends, relatives, acquaintances—and in turn their's, etc. that might subsequently be referred to your office). _____

PERSON-TO-PERSON PUBLIC RELATIONS

Public relations in its simplest form is nothing more than "human relations"; it embodies warmth, understanding, kindness and concern for others—on a person-to-person basis.

For some individuals, this is easy: a flashing smile, a twinkle in the eyes, a natural empathy that comes through quickly and easily. For others possibly lacking these characteristics, it is simply a matter of a little extra effort to make sure these genuine qualities shine through in other ways.

Sometimes just a couple of words can make the difference.

Those two little words "thank you" are a lot more than a mere expression of gratitude which makes the other person feel better. They also help the other person to "do better" and tend to cause him to repeat the response that brought the "thank you." The psychologists call it "reinforcement."

One reason a "thank you" is such a powerful reinforcer is that gratitude itself is an "extra," a bonus—not the standard routine *sad* to say. Unfortunately people who feel appreciation seldom express it. They feel it inside, but for some reason they get inhibited, forgetful, or just plain busy and never let it out.

Dr. Herbet M. Greenberg, a corporate consultant on fitting individuals to their jobs, explains that one reason "thank you" is a rarity these days is: Most working people dislike their jobs and, in fact, don't belong in them.

Watch people on their way to work, he says. Stand on a street corner in the morning and watch them go by. They look down in the mouth. They're cranky and grumbly, like they really did not want to get up and go to work.

You can understand why, in private life, you come up against such rudeness today. Taxi drivers slam the door in your face if your destination doesn't suit their plans, clerks turn away from your problems, and repair people go through the motions like they couldn't care less.

"Service with a smile" is now *no service with a shrug*," and today the customer is always wrong. It seems like everybody has the "blaaahs."

Well we're not going to change the world with a "thank you." But we're going to fill a vacuum. Our "thank you" will fall like rain in a desert wilderness. And human nature will love us for it.

So let other people know how *you* feel. Don't take it for granted that they know you appreciate them. Tell them. When you let people know you appreciate what they have done, it makes them want to do still more for you.

HOW TO MULTIPLY THE POWER OF HUMAN RELATIONS

In Chapter 5 we said "resist the usual" in setting the stage for practice growth. It applies even more to human relations.

Here's a case in point where the "usual" almost seems like an affront:

Many practitioners use pre-printed "thank you" cards to acknowledge referrals. They fill certain blank spaces provided by the printer and perfunctorily send these cards out when they are not too busy. It's a "thank you" to be sure, but it's cold, impersonal, mass-produced, and lacks any special meaning—at least to the recipient.

As Les Giblin says in his best-selling *How to Have Confidence and Power in Dealing with People*,* no girl likes to receive carbon copies of a love letter, and everyone wants the kind of treatment which seems to say "This is especially for you."

Referrals from "enthusiastic" P/Cs and colleagues not only pay you the supreme compliment of confidence, but also make possible the growth and development of your practice. Can there be any reason under the sun to take them "for granted" or to tell the secretary to handle them in the "usual way?"

"The most destructive force in the world," writes Edward Kramer founder of the Kimball Foundation of Human Engineering, "is the 'take-it-for-granted' habit. Love taken for granted is love lost. Life taken for granted is life made lifeless. The

---

* L. Giblin, *How to Have Confidence and Power in Dealing with People* (Prentice-Hall, Englewood Cliffs, N.J., 1956).

senses become dull and jaded. Soon days are lost in uneventful dullness. The events are there but you are not."

Here are some unusual ideas for giving thanks that will increase your awareness of the good that others do and multiply your power of human relations and the pleasure of others—on both personal and professional levels:

1) Thank your referral sources *promptly* with a personal word or better yet a personal note. A few handwritten words on a small card has even more meaning and remembrance value than the "standard" letter typed by a secretary. Many practitioners I know make this a "happy habit" at the end of each day.

2) In *The $100,000 Practice and How To Build It,* I showed a picture of a "Thank-U-Gram" originated by the aforementioned Dr. Kramer. It is a small, yellow form similar to a telegram, and used to mail out a personal message of gratitude.*

Many practitioners find these easy-to-use forms ideal for acknowledging referrals and always appreciated by those who receive them.

Here are some additional uses for them.

Why wait until Christmas to thank those who provide service to you and your family throughout the year. Do it when it's unexpected and your "thanks" will be more noticeable and more meaningful than during the deluge of holiday cards. Include your staff, your colleagues, your suppliers, the gals at the answering service, the postman, the barber, the waitress at your neighborhood coffee shop. Go the full route.

For good measure, add a "smile button" in appreciation of good service.

Don't bet against this idea. There are few situations where human nature doesn't work reciprocally. You'll literally get "service with a smile" in the future because you're letting other people know they're appreciated.

A New Jersey practitioner told me it got his building's elevator operator smiling for the first time in ten years!

3) In the business world, they say the sweetest words in the world are "check enclosed," but even these can be improved with a small embellishment. A Texas practitioner, when sending checks to suppliers and local tradesmen, inserts them in a printed folder that reads: "It's a pleasure to send you the enclosed check." And his name is printed below this warm message.

A Bangor, Maine practitioner varied this idea by having the local bank print his checks so they now read: *"It's a pleasure to*—pay to the order of _____."
It required only four additional words to the "usual" form.

An Iowa practitioner adds only *two* words to all in-coming checks. They are: "Thank you" above his endorsement.

Human concern knows no bounds, geographical or otherwise. And most of the time, it takes such little effort to express it that I'm constantly amazed why more people don't try it.

4) The "graduate" thank you is a *second* note of appreciation sent many months or even years after the original one. It can tell friends how much you are still enjoying a gift they sent. It can be written to someone who gave you a "helping hand" in the

---

* Write Kimball Foundation, Brentwood, Missouri 63144 for further information about "Thank-U-Grams."

early days of your practice or to a former college professor whose advice served you well.

If you were to take stock right now of all the nice things that have been given to you, or done for you—for which you have already expressed your appreciation once—you would probably find that you are still enjoying a number of them.

Why not multiply the power of your human relations, and the pleasure of others, by sending a *second* note of thanks?

5) Here is still another variation. It's the "in-depth" way of saying "thank you." It is specific and mentions some detail that makes the other person feel even better than the "usual" acknowledgment.

To your wife: "The pie was delicious; the crust was so flaky" is the extra embellishment that proves personal appreciation.

To a member of your staff: "Thanks for handling this afternoon's rush at the office so well. You certainly have a warm, friendly way of dealing with people."

To a colleague: "Thanks for referring Mrs. Smith. Your covering report was most thorough and helpful."

While general statements of appreciation may cover the etiquette of the situation, they fall far short of the opportunity to give the *extra* pleasure that a small embellishment adds.

If these examples sound low-pitch to you, then I rejoice. For this is a sure sign your own brand of human relations is about to sprout.

Let it come forth. And if you feel uncomfortable about it, then know this discomfort may be due to cracks in the ivory tower.

It may seem a far cry from a "thank you" to a more successful practice. Yet to the technically perfect practitioner, it may be a new path to practice growth.

TO MAKE THE WORLD A BETTER PLACE

Leaders in all fields recognize that there are responsibilities that go hand-in-hand with business operations. Dan Seymour, President of the large advertising firm J. Walter Thompson, put it this way: "You can no longer run your business simply by making and selling a product. You must consider the consequences of your business, what it does to human beings and for human beings."

The highest form of public relations is available in all professions and to all practitioners. It extends beyond discipline and knows no geographical bounds. It is the purest form of public service and immune from ethical reproach.

It is making the world a better place to live in.

It could mean stopping for a child to cross the street or it could mean campaigning against air pollution.

It could mean counselling a friend or joining the Peace Corps.

It could mean donating a pint of blood to the Red Cross.

It most definitely does mean listening to the still voice of conscience and expressing it in outward action—action aimed at bringing the society of man to a higher level.

What has this got to do with practice growth?

Everything. The world is very small. There is no place left to hide. If we want a world to practice in, we must work for it and be part of it.

And the world depends on its professional people to be a most important part.

8

How to Upgrade
Your P/Cs' Thinking

About 150 years after Goethe said, "Treat people as they were what they ought to be and you help them to become what they are capable of being," Harvard psychologist Robert Rosenthal was discovering that grade school teachers who were led to expect more of certain students found that these children gained as many as 15 to 27 I.Q. points over their classmates whose learning abilities were thought to be just "average." The only difference between the students was in the attitudes of the teachers. Because the teachers had been led to expect more of these supposedly "gifted" students, these children came to expect more of themselves. Their performance seemed to follow as a result.

"The explanation probably lies in the subtle interaction between teacher and pupils," reports Rosenthal. "Tone of voice, facial expression, touch and posture may be the means by which, often unwittingly, she communicates her expectations to her pupils. Such communication may help a child by changing his perceptions of himself."

Writing about these studies in the *Reader's Digest*, John Kord Lagemann has said: "The knowledge that others believe in us and are counting on us acts as a self-fulfilling prophecy and helps us to become as good as they think we are." *

The "self-fulfilling prophecy" amounts to a "you can do it" philosophy, an expression of confidence in others. These expectations bring out the best in people and they tend to respond favorably to those who have this confidence in them.

It works in the classroom, in the sports world, at home, and in the business and professional office.

A P/C, during a visit to a professional practice, is in a learning situation regarding his "problem," what caused it, what should be done about it, and his ability to cope with it. His comprehension, his cooperation, even his "performance" can be influenced by the practitioner's actions, attitudes and expectations.

HOW TO RAISE THE P/Cs' SERVICE I.Q.

In Chapter 3, a "practice" was described as a heterogeneous "group of individuals" with P/Cs divided into four categories. The A, B, C, and D classifications were used to describe different levels of understanding and appreciation of complete professional services (Service I.Q.), with "A" representing the best-informed and motivated type and "D," at the opposite end of the scale, representing the least informed and cooperative type.

Most P/Cs' thinking can be upgraded, their Service I.Q. changed for the better. It requires only a willingness to do it (an "I Care Attitude"), a basic confidence in the P/C, and a few simple tested principles of P/C education. This chapter summarizes some of the proven methods used by successful practitioners.

Specific examples from varied professions are intended to give a broader perspective on this subject. Hopefully, if some of the ideas do not seem applicable to your particular profession, they will still be meaningful to you as a patient or client in another field. In the latter case, by seeing how easily your thinking can be changed once a few facts are known, you may feel differently about the desirability and feasibility of applying these methods in your own practice.

COMMUNICATION IS A TWO-WAY STREET

Effective communication requires a consideration of not only *what* is said but, even more importantly, the P/C's *interpretation* of what is said.

It may be different.

The practitioner at the outset is at a disadvantage because his past experiences and everyday use of professional terminology tend to make many words and phrases commonplace in his vocabulary. Under these circumstances, it is easy for him to take these expressions for granted and to assume that the meaning is also clear to the P/C.

Technically, his words may be correct. But, if they have acquired meanings that

---

* John Kord Lagemann, "Self-Fulfilling Prophecy—A Key to Success," *Reader's Digest,* February, 1969.

are not on target, if the P/C's interpretation is different than intended, a breakdown in communications occurs.

For example, in the health-care professions, the word "surgery"—even when referring to minor surgery—sets up in the minds of many people a frightening, anxiety-laden, life-and-death situation. Its negative connotations can deter P/C acceptance and consent. In discussing *minor* surgery, these inferences and reactions are unjustified and unnecessary, by definition. What many practitioners say instead is "minor procedures."

By the same token, the words "injection" and "medication" have a more positive and acceptable connotation than the sometimes thoughtlessly used terms "shot" and "drugs."

An interesting discovery we have made in our veterinary surveys concerns the expression "practice limited to small animals," which is occasionally found on professional letterheads or in the telephone book. Surprisingly enough, some clients take it literally and conclude that the veterinarian, in this case, will not treat a *large* dog.

Words can become out-of-date and worn from use and practitioners in all professions are recognizing the psychological value of words that touch off positive emotions. For example, in the law profession, the term "divorce lawyer," is being superceded by "practitioners of family law."

Many practitioners refer to the women members of their staff as "the girls." No disrespect is intended but in the P/C's eyes, it downgrades the assistants' professional competence and in turn, leads some P/Cs to the erroneous conclusion that the staff has been considered of "non-professional" status. Delegation of responsibility, in this instance, becomes difficult. In the assistant's eyes, it downgrades her job skills and, if she is sensitive, her morale as well.

To refer to assistants as "lay help" (or P/Cs as "laymen") is ITA compounded by "snobbery." It's one term that is really out-of-date.

How about the term "professional assistant" or some other appropriate title followed by the person's name? Surnames engender more respect, if not formality, than first names. Many consider this more dignified and appropriate.

Many practitioners refer to an assistant as "office manager," which simplifies fee discussions and appointment scheduling when they are delegated. By delegating *authority* as well as responsibility in such matters, it obviates the interruptions (and embarrassment to the assistant) caused by the P/C who feels a more favorable decision will be made by the practitioner.

An Akron, Ohio veterinarian refers to his "kennel boy" as "kennel director" and he does his work more proudly than if he went unrecognized and unappreciated.

It amounts to nothing more than the "human touch."

Some professional words need to be simplified and reduced to more meaningful terms. The fields of law, insurance, accounting, and real estate abound with them. Even such an innocuous term as "loophole," meaning in the vernacular of these professions a legal technicality, has been thought by some clients to mean something a trifle shady, if not downright dishonest.

Perceptive practitioners prefer to call a "loophole" an "exception" or "legal relief." It certainly puts a legitimate tax-saving, not to mention the practitioner's integrity, in a different light for those who might otherwise misinterpret these provisions.

Some professional words, because of over-use, need changing to convey greater impact. For example, in the eye-care professions, some patients have been told, for the sake of simplicity, that they are a "little near-sighted" or have "20/40 vision."

These expressions may be technically correct, but they tend to *oversimplify* the true extent of vision loss. If these terms are *interpreted* casually as "nothing serious," then the patient may be lulled into a false sense of complacency, or worse, an attitude of indifference towards the importance of wearing corrective lenses and having periodic re-examinations.

Many practitioners convert these visual acuity findings into more meaningful expressions—such as "a 25% loss of vision" or "only 75% of clear vision"—not to scare the patient, but to furnish additional information of motivational value.

Is this now *over*stating the case?

Would the perspective be any different if you considered the prospect of driving along a two-lane highway with another car approaching at 60 miles an hour and driven by a person with "uncorrected vision?"

Food for thought: Can your findings, diagnosis, or progress report be described in terms that are even more meaningful and motivational to the P/C?

HOW TO TELL A COMPLETE STORY

I would guess the briefest correspondence in history transpired when a British author, wondering how the sales of his latest book were going, sent the editor a letter containing the single notation: "?"

The editor's equally terse reply was: "!"

This was a "complete story."

In dealing with others, sometimes just "the facts" are enough. At other times, especially when we want to conjure up savory images and touch off positive emotions, additional details are required. Often, all that's needed is the "human touch."

"Homemade apple pie" on a restaurant menu has been proved to outsell "apple pie" by many times.

"Kentucky Fried Chicken" states the facts about the nationally-known creation of Colonel Sanders, but the slogan "It's finger-lickin' good" creates a "word picture" that captures the imagination.

And imagination is the trigger of desire.

Several years ago, five real estate brokers in New Jersey tried without success for three months to sell a home with basically this advertisement:

Piscataway—Lake Nelson. 6 room ranch with fireplace, garage, tile bath, oil-hot water heat. Convenient to Rutgers campus, stadium, golf courses and primary schools. $18,000.

Using the "personal touch" the homeowner's wife wrote her own ad, which pulled six prospects, one of whom bought the next day. It read:

Piscataway—Lake Nelson, north side. We'll miss our house. We've been comfortable in it, but 2 bedrooms aren't enough for us, so we must move. If you like to be cozy by a fire while you admire autumn woods through wide windows, protected from the street; if you like a shady yard in summer, a clear view of winter sunsets and quiet enough to hear frogs in spring, but want city utilities and conveniences, you might like to buy our house. We hope so. We don't want it empty and alone at Christmas. The price is flexible.

Professional men who take the time to tell a P/C the complete story are supplying the quintessence of a humanized practice and providing a "booster rocket" to a higher level of P/C understanding and appreciation.

Here are some additional tips:

Time. Take all the time you think you need to "get through" but pay the law of diminishing returns its due respect. Identical explanations used for the same procedure, but to different P/Cs, need a different amount of time and patience, just as photograph film needs varying times of exposure depending on sensitivity.

Steps. Tell the story in increments, not all at once. For example, tell the P/C all the pertinent facts during any one visit; but, where a long-range program is involved, spread your education and motivational efforts over a series of visits if you wish to elevate that Service I.Q.

Involve the P/C. Educators have discovered that learning is . . .

    1% by taste,

    1½% by touch,

    3½% by smell,

    11% by hearing,

    83% by sight.

They have demonstrated that combinations of two or more sensory channels can extend the retention of learning manyfold.

When information is communicated by "telling" only, the recall three hours later is approximately 70%; three days later, it is only 10%.

On the other hand, when this same information is "shown" to the individual, three hours later the recall is 72%; three days later, it is some 35%.

When the two methods of communication are combined ("showing and telling"), the recall three hours later is 85%; three days later; it is 65%!

Let the P/C participate in the education process by using *both* verbal and visual communication. Some examples are:

Aids: Use visual aids, including charts, diagrams, x-rays, take-apart anatomical models, to increase comprehension and recall.

You can create your own visual aids informally and spontaneously. Often a well-prepared, standardized presentation may be so handsomely illustrated that it is too "slick" for its own good. The fact that the P/C knows it has been designed to facilitate acceptance may cause a subconscious resistance.

You may communicate more effectively with an "ad lib" sketch. Spontaneity and the personal touch often add just the right note of authenticity and sincerity to hold the P/C's attention and respect. Created in the presence of the P/C, they invest the case presentation with freshness and seeming originality. You can make your rough visualizations without artistic talent. In fact, their unprofessional, homespun character is the key to their believability.

Example 1

The securities salesman may draw a rough chart like this to illustrate the general investment principle. In this case, the investment dollar is suspended by three springs to the sides of a triangle representing "safety," "yield," and "chance for growth." In a well-balanced security, the investment opportunities for all three are reasonably assured. In a security currently yielding more income, the chances are the investment dollar will tend to move away from "safety" and "chance for growth."

Example 2

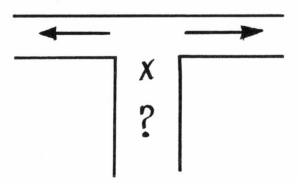

This simple diagram can be used to illustrate three alternatives: long-range preventive maintenance programs that prevent trouble, short-term palliative stop-gap programs that merely cope with trouble temporarily, and the third possibility of doing nothing—and risking the problem of further complications and backsliding.

Another valuable communications tool is the analogy. A parallel created with something familiar to the P/C—an example in his job or home life—has the effect of translating your language into his.

Often what makes perfect, crystal-clear sense to the practitioner has no meaning or significance for the P/C until it is interpreted through the use of analogy.

Dentists have compared the teeth to a set of tools, to illustrate their separate functions.

Dr. Joseph Bregstein, DDS * of New York, explains it this way: Your front teeth are called incisors because they act like scissors to cut the food. Your cuspids are like pliers because they tear the food to shreds. Then your bicuspids act like a nutcracker to break the food into smaller segments. Finally, your molars grind the food like a mortar and pestle. Every one of these tools has a specific job, and you need every one to eat properly. If you don't replace one missing tool, you force some other tool to do its job. Did you ever try to mash walnuts with a scissors or cut steak with a nutcracker?

HOW TO ADD "DRAMA"
TO YOUR PROFESSIONAL MESSAGE

Here are some examples to illustrate how "visual impact" can enhance P/C education:

1) At the Arkansas Baptist Medical Center in Little Rock, there is a "Play Hospital" area, which local kindergarten children visit to learn about hospital life. These children get more than just a hospital tour. One of them, for example, is chosen to be a "patient" destined for a tonsillectomy. Classmates watch as the "patient" goes through all the "procedures" including admittance, lab tests, pre-examination and actual "play operation." Then each child gets a sack containing a sample of things they have seen in the Play Hospital—cotton balls, a toy syringe, tongue depressor, identification bracelet, etc. The Play Hospital is an enjoyable and educational experience for the youngsters. The hospital believes that it has helped some of these children make a good adjustment for the time when they may have to come to the real hospital for treatment.

Is a "dry run" or "mock visit" appropriate for your profession? Would it help P/Cs for future visits?

2) A Missouri attorney takes a client with a pending case into the courtroom when it's in session to show where the judge and jury sit and what the courtroom procedures are. It takes the strangeness and fright out of a first-time appearance, especially for a client who has never before faced an audience or been confronted by an ominous black-robed judge and the skeptical stares of twelve jurors. He gives the client a set of "Pointers for Witnesses."

These are extras that not only upgrade the client's Service I.Q. but also demonstrate the "I Care Attitude" of his legal counselor.

3) An Illinois dentist uses a phase microscope to let his patients see a scraping taken from the necks of their teeth with the bacteria in frantic action. It helps them understand the decay process and the value of periodic dental care.

---

* Dr. Joseph Bregstein, *Interviewing, Counseling, and Managing Dental Patients* (Prentice-Hall, Inc., Englewood Cliffs, N.J., 1957).

A Florida veterinarian lets clients view, through a simple miscroscope, the intestinal worms that plague their pets to help them appreciate the importance of routine worming procedures.

The personal involvement in these cases engages and activates the P/C's self-interest. The added "drama" produces a "seeing is believing" reaction that helps to overcome P/C neglect and apathy. Preventive maintenance "comes to life" through the use of visual impact.

4) Most physicians attending patients in the hospital fill out their reports after completing "rounds," usually at the nurses' station. There, they will conscientiously study x-rays and lab reports, write up progress reports and nurses' orders. Yet, their patients often complain how little time the doctor spends on their case.

A Boston internist has an answer to this problem. He does as much paper work as possible right at the patient's bedside, including (when appropriate) a phone call to the lab or consultant on the case. These extra, personal efforts provide patient education and peace of mind, and project an image of a more attentive, concerned practitioner.

5) A west coast realtor makes video tape recordings of selected properties with a battery-operated, shoulder-carried unit and hand camera. Views are taken of both interiors and exteriors. These are then shown to prospective buyers in the office. The system saves time for the prospect, the realtor, and the seller whose privacy is not invaded by prospects. It has reduced the realtor's staff, having eliminated the need for his representatives to combine driving and entertaining with selling. It has created a more professional image for the broker in relationships with both customer and the client. It has enabled the broker to give sellers a "bird's eye view" of the market in general, thus establishing a realistic figure for his property at the outset, without the necessity of taking him on a tour of a dozen or more properties for a comparison with his own.

6) Instead of going through long, repetitive oral explanations or routine instructions, many practitioners are utilizing motion picture films, with color and sound, live animation, and narration to tell their "story."

Made by commercial firms under professional supervision, these films are available in snap-in cartridges that can be used with portable, push-button projectors.

Alternatives are film strips with records or tape recordings, either commercially-made or homemade. Aside from an appreciable saving of time, these audio-visual aids effectively tell the *complete* story, each and every time. They can be used to convert "waiting" time into a purposeful experience that upgrades the P/C's Service I.Q. They can "plant the seed" for future services and/or prepare the P/C for a future event.

TELL YOUR PROFESSIONAL MESSAGE BY BROCHURE

Many offices, hoping to *prevent* trouble rather than just cope with it, have printed literature that spells out the importance of preventive care and the professional philosophy of the practitioner. Such literature is also helpful in delineating office policies regarding appointments, fees, telephone consultations, services offered (or not offered), office hours, house calls, or any other P/C privileges or obligations.

Office policy not known by the P/C is often policy ignored. "I'm sorry; it's office policy" is a totally unsatisfactory response to an uninformed P/C. Some typical titles of printed policies I have seen are:

—"Our Policy Regarding Service, Fees and Retainers"
—"The Preventive Maintenance Treatment—The Philosophy of This Office"
—"An Introduction to Our Philosophy of Group Practice"
—"An Introduction to Our Office Policies for Patients Who Have Never Been Treated Here Before"

For hospital-bound patients, the Orange County Medical Association (California) has prepared for its members a brochure that begins: "Medical and hospital expenses are seldom welcomed, but knowing in advance what to expect and how to plan for them, can lessen the burden. We hope this brochure will assist you in planning for your hospitalization."

Among the items that are briefly discussed in this brochure are: the surgery schedule (day of admittance, date of surgery, and the estimated duration of hospital stay); professional fees and estimate of the approximate range of fees for the surgeon, assistant surgeon, and anesthesiologist; post-operative care; health insurance (for those who have it and for those who don't); instructions and information (prior to hospitalization and after it); and employee disability benefits.

Such brochures usually are written very informally, with a view to communicating and informing on a friendly basis. For example, here is the style of a New York hospital brochure: "To you, our guest . . . a word of welcome. This may be your first visit as a patient in the Boulevard Hospital, or you may be an old friend returning for another visit. In either case we will do our utmost to make your stay here pleasant and beneficial. We are dedicated to the optimum in patient care and we welcome your opinions and suggestions. Best wishes for a speedy recovery."

Still another advantage of a printed policy is that sticky problems can be carefully worded and expressed more diplomatically than random, "off the cuff" explanations. From the success files, here are six examples:

—From a veterinary hospital: "The management of this hospital corresponds to that of a human hospital in that all business must be conducted on a cash basis."
—"Insurance policies are contracts between you, the subscriber and the company. The doctor can in no way alter the policy nor guarantee your payments. Each company pays different rates for similar services. Some insurance plans may seem identical but have riders that alter the fee schedule."
—For appointment cards: "If unable to keep this reservation PLEASE give 24 hours notice so that another patient may use your time. No charge will be made if adequate notice is given."
—"Occasionally our regular fees are reduced based on individual or family circumstances. Requests for reduced fees will always receive careful, sympathetic and confidential consideration."

—"Because my employees now share with me proportionately in the proceeds of this practice, it is no longer my privilege to write 'No Charge' in regard to any particular patient, no matter how friendly our relationship." . . . with an optional paragraph, if appropriate, as follows: "However, all of us still take pleasure in allowing courtesy reduction, and this is reflected in the net charges made."

—"We can quote a fixed fee for standardized services, such as the drafting of routine deeds and wills or the initiating of a simple, corporate organization. In some cases, our fee is fixed by the courts or by law. But in most matters, for example a court action, it is generally impossible for us to predict in advance how much time and attention will be required. Because of these uncertainties, it is more proper and fairer to avoid a fixed fee in advance. We shall be pleased, however, to furnish you with an idea of the fees charged in similar cases which can be but rough estimates of what we believe our fee will be if no complications or unforeseen circumstances occur."

Tip: Many practitioners, in preparing their own brochures, include a section pertaining to the P/C's personal record. It is filled in at the time of the office visit and includes current status, and any other pertinent data from the case record, of interest or value to the P/C for future reference (for example while on a trip). In addition to the convenience it affords the P/C, this personal record is an incentive for the P/C to retain this educational folder.

WHERE TO FIND "SOURCE MATERIALS" FOR TAKE-HOME LITERATURE

Most professions have association-written and approved literature that explains in well-illustrated, easy-to-understand terms, the background, objectives, requirements, functions and areas of service of their particular profession. Some offer pamphlets that describe specific situations, facts or warning signs that would indicate the need for professional attention. Some stress preventive measures. Still others take the "mystery" out of certain professional procedures that have caused unfounded fears, apprehensions, and anxieties which have actually kept people from seeking professional advice.

Many business firms catering to the professions have developed well-written institutional brochures designed to help practitioners with the job of P/C education. Textbooks and journals offer a wealth of information.

These items can be rewritten, reprinted, or used as is to suit your needs and the interests of your P/Cs.

REPETITION MAY TURN THE TRICK

If you are not getting through to a P/C, it is natural to blame it on P/C procrastination. As mentioned earlier, though procrastination has no advocates, it has a lot of friends. However, there may be another factor at work—*inertia.*

Inertia is an enemy of the successful practice.

P/C inertia can be overcome only by more massive doses of motivation. You can increase the dose by using it in a more potent form. We have already covered ways to do this with various forms of communication.

You can also increase the dose by repeating it.

Are you cautious about repeating the benefits and advantages of what you are recommending? Then you need to remind yourself of the value to the P/C of following your advice.

It is not unprofessional to remind repeatedly. Once, twice, three times may not be enough.

In the advertising world, there's an adage that an advertiser's message doesn't get through until the fifth repetition. Also, there's a saying among salesmen that 85 percent of sales are made on the fifth try. But 85 percent of salesmen don't make a fifth call. They give up before that.

The psychologists have proven the "magic" of five repetitions. In "Modes of Emphasis in Public Speaking" by A.T. Jersild in the *Journal of Applied Psychology* (1928, published by the American Psychological Association, 12:611–620), one criterion of the effectiveness with which you have put across a number of ideas is how many are remembered. Also, if you influence people only momentarily, it is a rather futile activity. To be worthwhile, your influence must be lasting.

Jersild studied the effectiveness of various devices in public speaking to determine how they aided memory of specific facts by the audience. To test this, he prepared a short biography of a fictitious individual and memorized it. He then presented it orally to ten different classes in a large university. The speech was so arranged that the order of ideas could be changed, as well as the obvious variations in inflection, gesture, etc. A particular phrase might, in one class, be emphasized by banging on the desk; in another, by preceding it with the admonition, "now get this"; or in another, by speaking more loudly, etc.

The results for some devices are shown in the table. In this table, 100% means the memory value of a fact when it was in the middle of the speech and not emphasized.

Effect of Various Emphasis Devices upon
Memory for Specific Facts (from Jersild 1928)

Device	% Score
5 repetitions	315
4 repetitions	246
3 repetitions	197
now get this	191
primacy	175
did you notice that	154
pause	143
loudness	126
gesture	118
bang	115
unemphasized middle of speech	100
slow speech	79

Putting a particular idea right at the beginning increases its memory value by 75%, as is shown by its percentage score of 175. The table shows that repetition is not more effective than other devices until we get up to three repetitions of a fact. The specific warning "now get this" increases memory value 91%, whereas calling attention to a fact after giving it is better by only 54% than the unemphasized version of the same fact.

It seems pretty clear from this study that important ideas should be presented first—that you should go straight to your main point. Then repeat it four times.

Pertinent data must be emphasized. Such tricks as pausing before important points, raising the voice, banging on a table, or gesturing with the hand and arm have great value in increasing the memory value of significant points. Greater than any of these is the adept use of signpost phrases such as "now get this," or in terms more appropriate for a professional office: "Here is an important point."

It is interesting to note that an exaggerated slowing down of speech is negative in its effect on memory. Statements so "emphasized" were remembered less well than when delivered at the ordinary rate without emphasis.

WHAT TO DO WHEN ALL ELSE FAILS

Some P/Cs are obstinate, hard-headed and difficult to reach through ordinary educational channels.

Telling won't teach them, because they're not listening.

Showing won't teach them, because they won't read.

Worst of all, some of them readily admit they're not doing the right thing by continuing to neglect professional attention and preventive maintenance.

How do you reach them?

Many have found that the "light touch" works wonders. A dash of humor, instead of a sermon, finally penetrates the listening-learning barrier.

The American Cancer Society's recent "humorous" campaign against cigarette smoking has been more effective in reducing cigarette consumption than all the statistics and sermons of years gone by.

The Connecticut Highway Commission's "humorous" poster campaign against speeding has reduced auto accidents more than "radar warnings."

Training films for Army personnel have been proven to communicate and educate more effectively with a smile instead of a shout.

Much of today's advertising evidences the "soft sell" and "light touch" approach. Its realism and remembrance value have been shown to be enhanced.

Here are two examples of hand-out literature from professional practice that may give you an idea to try as a change of pace or as an alternative with an occasional P/C:

FOOD FOR THOUGHT

It really doesn't bother me,   yet.

(an idea from the office of: Jerome S. Mittelman, D.D.S., New York, N. Y.)

BARGAIN HUNTING?

Beware of bargains in
>   Parachutes
>   life preservers
>   fire extinguishers
>   brain operations and
>   foot care

SUMMARY

Communications fail to occur for many reasons. The most important reason is the language barrier—not the foreign language barrier, but the professional language barrier. Another reason is the *gap*—not necessarily the generation gap, but the professional-P/C gap. A break in communications for any reason can be critical to P/C and practitioner, so every technique in the book must be used to keep lines open—audio-visual, drama, brochure, repetition, the "light touch," multi-media, etc. The results are worth it.

Here are the alternatives to consider:

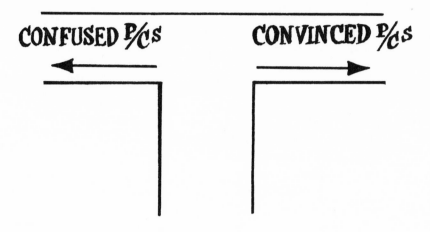

9

The Convincing
Case Presentation

A few years ago, the Cream of Wheat company had an ad called "Breakfast Surprise." It was aimed at the parents who have ever struggled to get their children to eat a hot, nourishing breakfast.

In a full page of tempting color, the ad featured a bowl of hot Cream of Wheat with a scoop of strawberry ice cream!

In part, the copy read: "It takes *ideas* to keep kids interested in breakfast."

It set me thinking. Doesn't it also take ideas to keep P/Cs interested in professional services, to overcome their indifference and apathy, and to motivate them to "want" the care and advice they also need?

The object of a thorough and effective case presentation, with verbal and visual explanations, is to do just that. It is to communicate what you know—to P/Cs so as to insure a high level of comprehension, motivation and cooperation—for their benefit.

We've set the climate of understanding for case presentation. Here are some additional tested ideas for maintaining a high level of P/C interest.

1) *Talk the P/C's language.* Several years ago, I was allowed to observe a case presentation made by a North Carolina practitioner to an older woman patient.

"After a thorough and careful evaluation of the test findings . . .," I heard him begin. He then went on with a very professional presentation of his findings, analysis, and recommendations. To the best of my ability to judge, it was textbook perfect, well-organized and delivered without a flaw.

In fact, midway through it, he glanced toward me with an expression that I interpreted as meaning: "Isn't this sensible and convincing?"

My expression confirmed that it was.

And the patient also seemed to be "taking it all in," nodding in agreement, and going along with the recommendations.

However, I thought to myself that, crystal-clear and convincing as it was to *him*, textbook-perfect though it may have been, it was also in textbook *language*. If the patient was having half the difficulty that I was in following him, she'd be hopelessly confused.

When the "moment of truth" and affirmation did arrive, the patient hesitated a moment and said, "I'll think it over and call you."

After she left, he turned to me and said, "You can see for yourself. This is a difficult area. These people are different. How can you fight ignorance and apathy?"

It wasn't his "area." It wasn't the "people." It wasn't even his "ability." The obstacle to communication and agreement, in this case, was his "attitude."

He was simply taking too much for granted.

The patient's "need" was there. He had undoubtedly "diagnosed" it correctly and knew how to "solve" it. His problem in this case (and it became the patient's problem as well) was that he simply wasn't talking the patient's language.

The result was predictable. The human mind just cannot act favorably on what it does not understand.

The simple difference between the "confused" P/C and the "convinced" P/C is a matter of *communication—in terms meaningful to the P/C.*

The Allstate Insurance Company has recognized this principle in a brochure entitled "Plain Talk." In part, it says: "Once you part the ivy and slice through the gobbledegook, insurance suddenly stops being so confusing . . . Allstate Agents speak a simple, un-insurance lingo a man can understand."

2) *Have empathy for the other person's point of view.* In order to talk P/Cs' language, it is necessary to understand their perspective—or lack of perspective, as the case may be. In a word, it requires empathy.

Empathy is the ability to relate to other people, to identify with them, to feel as they do. It allows one to perceive intuitively what the other person is thinking and to understand the psychology of his needs.

The great French aviator and writer Antoine de Saint Exupery said "Marriage is not looking at each other, but looking in the same direction together." And this is just as applicable to case presentation as it is to marriage. "It's not looking at each other, but looking in the same direction." It's an attitude that says in effect, "Your problem is my problem. Let's work on it together." It is the essence of empathy.

Empathy is sometimes confused with sympathy, but this is a very different psychological process. You can understand what a person is thinking and feeling (empathy) without necessarily agreeing with him (sympathy). For example, a practitioner can understand his P/C's fears and hesitations without (tacitly) agreeing to postpone the work or to compromise his recommendations. In fact, "feeling sorry" for the P/C, especially where postponement or compromise will aggravate or compound the "problem," is misguided sympathy. Another man with equal empathy, but less sympathy, recognizes and appreciates his P/C's fears and hesitations, but takes the time and effort to help the P/C understand the consequences of further delay and/or benefits of proceeding immediately.

This process is one of communication and interaction between practitioner and P/C. It depends on the ability of each to "project" to the other, to convey his emotions, ideas and attitudes. Although ideally it is a two-way process, in most situations it is difficult for the P/C to project his true feelings because he is psychologically at a disadvantage in the typical professional office. He is out of his element in a world totally different from the one to which he is accustomed. The sights, the sounds, the people are unfamiliar, bewildering, perhaps frightening. Notwithstanding his authority and position in the "outside world," his role in the professional office becomes one of submission to practitioner and staff. Furthermore, he is "trapped" by a situation over which he has no control (e.g., poor health or legal troubles, unexpected and unwelcomed expenses, loss of time or wages, inconvenience, embarrassment or something far worse). The seeds of bitterness, resentment, and negativity are there.

The costs of professional services are often defended (for the P/C's benefit) by comparing them with what the public spends for clothing, automobiles or just "a night on the town," but I think this is like trying to compare vacations and vaccinations. One is a discretionary, pleasure-producing expenditure while the other is an unwelcomed expense for something people wish they didn't need.

In the final analysis, many professional services are tantamount to "repair bills" in order to get something back in "working-order" or to solve problems that people wish hadn't arisen in the first place.

For the P/C in this frame of mind, receptivity, agreement, let alone enthusiasm, do not come easily.

If at the same time the practitioner appears cold, callous, indifferent, bored or hurried, his "attitude" will create additional emotional blocks for the P/C and further interfere with communication and agreement.

The responsibility thus rests on the practitioner to open up the lines of communication by properly "setting the stage"—environmentally and psychologically—to dispel all (unspoken) fears and emotional blocks, to listen attentively and perceivingly during the case history or other dialogues, to hear not only what the P/C says but *how* he says it. Only in this manner can the practitioner assess the P/C's attitudes, fears and pre-conceived ideas, and begin to evaluate his *total* needs—as a P/C *and* as a person.

Once the practitioner discovers his P/C's total needs, it is essential for him to now project *his* suggestions and recommendations to the P/C—in a way so as to insure co-operation and follow-through. This requires a warm, personal, and totally aligned case presentation. A lack of empathy at this time prevents the practitioner from correctly approaching the P/C to get agreement and consent. He will not likely know just what to say, how to say it, or when to say it. And he will be at a loss to evaluate the feedback the reluctant P/C gives him.

Empathy insures warmth and understanding by the practitioner, which is then reflected by the P/C. The result: more meaningful two-way communication, mutual understanding, rapport and acceptance.

Above all, empathy requires the *time* and *interest* in the P/C that only a quality-oriented practice can provide.

3) Monitor the P/C's understanding and comprehension. Don't take P/C comprehension for granted. Sometimes they think they understand, and they don't. Irrational though it may be, some try to fool you because they don't want to look stupid or because your "attitude" has inhibited them.

A good example of this is the question "Do you understand?" often asked by the practitioner at the conclusion of the case presentation. On paper, it looks innocuous enough, but when spoken this question has a tendency to sound belittling or condescending. Regardless of the sincerity of the practitioner, if it is *interpreted* that way by the P/C, it will be an inhibitor. The P/C will "clam up" and give tacit agreement—for the moment.

A far better question, that says the same thing but in a different way, is "Have I made myself clear?" It shows you are willing to accept at least part of the responsibility if the explanation has not been clear. It doesn't belittle the P/C or make him feel "dense" if he fails to grasp or completely understand your remarks. Asked in an unhurried, genuinely interested way, it demonstrates your concern and willingness to explain further if necessary. If there has been some ambiguity, the P/C will have no hesitation in saying so. You have let him "off the hook."

Another simple question that gives you the opportunity to monitor your P/C's understanding and comprehension is: "Is there anything you would like to discuss further?"

Many practitioners are afraid of this one, thinking it is a "loaded" question that will get them involved with other matters and only put them further behind schedule.

Is it worth the risk?

To the P/C, the question may come as a surprise, but always a pleasant one and a welcomed relief from the hurried ways of the "too busy to be bothered" type of practitioner. For some, it may supply a peace of mind for which there is no substitute.

This alone would warrant the question.

Those practitioners that do give the P/C an opportunity to ask questions and discuss the things uppermost in their minds say it is definitely worth the extra time, especially if their particular "professional plan" calls for a quality-oriented practice.

These extra few minutes often uncover new and unexpected aspects of the case, aspects which if ignored or glossed over could cause procrastination and drop-outs. ("Method of payment," "fear of the unknown" are subjects that, when left unanswered, often cause P/C procrastination and delay.)

At this point, a simple explanation may be all that is necessary. Take-home literature may offer further information or, if necessary, an extra appointment for the purpose of extended consultation may be arranged.

Is the value of the procedure not again a question of "To whom do you owe what?"

HOW TO INJECT P/Cs
WITH A MASSIVE DOSE OF MOTIVATION

It's been said you can lead a horse to water but you can't make him drink.

If you *first* make him "thirsty," the rest is easy.

This is the key to P/C motivation.

The authoritarian, high-pressure, demanding approach to influencing people is long out of date. Today's P/Cs are better educated and more sophisticated. This makes them more skeptical and more questioning.

But they still get thirsty.

Here, again, the emotions dominate.

People are governed by emotions, not logic. Their thoughts, actions and attitudes are dominated more by feelings than by reason.

P/Cs can be influenced by the application of stimuli calculated to stir the emotions. Telling is not teaching. Listening is not learning.

The failure of some college professors in "motivating" their students—and the success of football coaches with the same students—is due chiefly to reliance on "logic" in one case and "emotion" in the other.

Though it may seem bizarre, chocolate candies have been the key to successful education for several types of problem children when all else failed. Researchers at the Central Midwestern Regional Educational Laboratory have reported on this program of reinforcing good behavior and discouraging bad behavior. Rewards, begun as chocolate candies, progressed to tokens that could be exchanged for such privileges as a movie, a walk outside. The method has also worked to teach two-year-olds to read.

Emotions are seldom satisfied by negative motivators:

"Stop, Look, and Listen" signs mean little to people. Every day, people are hit by trains.

Since the law required cigarette packages to carry a health warning, the sale of cigarettes has steadily risen.

In the televised National Drivers Test of May 1965, 36 percent of the 26 million viewers did not know that a red blinking light means come to a full stop.

During World War II, the failure of people in England to take precautions from enemy bombing increased to serious proportions after every respite.

Psychologists explain that this indifference to seemingly remote eventualities is complicated by another tendency which might at first seem to offset it, but which actually reinforces it. It is the fear associated with the idea of accident, injury, disease and death. Such fear induces a negative attitude and a repression of the obvious consequences.

When you inform a P/C about the possibility of dire results, he develops a reluctance to even consider the possibilities of harm or delay.

The resistance to making a will or buying a burial plot is a combination of indifference to what is remote, and a negative block to what is unpleasant in favor of a profound optimism for the future.

It explains the illogical and irrational behavior of people who refuse to undergo an examination for fear it will disclose something bad. They maintain that, if anything is amiss, they don't want to know about it.

Then there are those P/Cs who are even more remote and more irrational. They deliberately withhold facts and information relevant to their case from the practitioner who is supposed to help them and to whom they are paying a fee. It may be amazing to the uninitiated, but it is well known to experienced practitioners that some people actually derive a feeling of satisfaction from purposely misleading and deceiving those whose advice they seek.

On occasion, the P/C's lack of cooperation is unconscious because of a psychological block. Physical therapists, for example, have told me of cases of paraplegics—those with motor and sensory paralysis of the entire lower half of their bodies—who would not "accept" their condition and the rehabilitation that was possible.

In the hearing-aid field, I have been told of people who similarly will just not "accept" their hearing loss.

Less obvious but still prevalent are the unrecognized needs for professional help in matters of accounting, law and insurance, to name a few areas where people tend to "shut their eyes" rather than face reality.

These "psychological blocks" can be overcome and are all the more reason for today's practitioner to "warm up" before he starts "pitching," to interact with the P/C so as to detect, if present, such blocks and—by inspiring faith, confidence and belief—to overcome them.

One of the most successful playwrights in the history of the American theatre was George M. Cohan. For years, every play he turned out had a scene in which the American flag was carried on stage or prominently displayed. This was his *positive* emotional stimulus.

You would not hear practitioner Cohan tell P/Cs that they were lazy or foolish for not following good advice. You would not hear him reprimand a late P/C when he finally arrived or bawl him out for neglect or procrastination. I don't know what his "brand of chocolate" might be, but you can bet he'd emphasize the positive. He'd find something to praise and something to reward.

A practitioner told me recently how he applied this reward concept to a patient who might have otherwise become discouraged and drop out. The case was a difficult one and, because of some unavoidable setbacks, a very time-consuming one. Nonetheless, the patient persevered, being very cooperative, understanding and helpful. At the right psychological moment, the practitioner showed the patient a bottle of the best champagne and said, "This will be your graduation present—with honors."

It certainly wasn't the champagne that made the patient's spirits soar. It was the act of recognition and appreciation of the patient's stick-to-it-iveness. It was not the gift so much as it was the gesture of respect and admiration.

It could have also been a Thank-U-Gram, a pat on the shoulder, a warm handshake, or just a compliment. It could have been anything that satisfied the emotions.

You get people to write a will, not by telling them of the dire consequences if they don't, but of the money their estate will save if they do and the "peace of mind" they will have knowing their affairs are in order.

You get people to wear hearing aids and eyeglasses, not by telling them they "should" or reprimanding them if they don't, but by motivating them with the idea that they will get "greater pleasure out of life," more classroom or job achievement, or other positive benefits.

You inspire people to have regular dental care, not by threats of cavities, decay, or loss of teeth, but by emphasizing youthful appearance, winning smiles, better digestion and "trouble-free teeth."

Remember the donkey. You'll never persuade her to pull a cart with a whip and a boot, but try holding grass in front of her.

You can motivate P/Cs beyond their ability to stand in the way by promise, not by threat. The P/C has a built-in circuit breaker that simply closes his mind to negative suggestions. He just does not listen.

Paint sunsets, not thunderclouds. Emphasize more comfort, better health, financial security, peace of mind, a better golf game or a better appearance—whatever the P/C's personal interest may be—and you have programmed a P/C for follow-through.

"GO" GOES FURTHER THAN "STOP"

Using the same psychological principle, appeals to action are far more effective than appeals to inhibition.

It is generally easier to get a person to do something than to get him to stop.

For example, with children, psychologists tell us that bad habits are most easily broken, not by saying "don't," but by substituting some other acceptable activity.

The P/C in a professional office is particularly vulnerable to criticism and resents being preached to, glared at, bawled out, threatened, snapped at and ridiculed.

The attempt to inhibit behavior with "don't do that" sets up, in effect, a head-on collision. To some people, it presents a kind of challenge. They are tempted to defy. Or the forbidden takes on an even greater attraction.

Like so many reactions of people, this is also illogical and irrational, especially if it is in the person's best interest to stop whatever he is doing, be it smoking, over-eating, procrastinating, or taking foolish chances. But it is emotional.

Fact: You can't neutralize emotion with logic. And the harder you try, the harder it becomes.

Motivate by exhorting to action. Tell how the action will benefit the P/C positively, appealing to emotional goals.

In *Between Parent and Child,* Dr. Hiam G. Ginott speaks of "The New Code of Communication." He explains that it is based on respect and on skill, requiring " (a) that messages preserve the child's as well as the parent's self respect; (b) that statements of understanding *precede* statements of advice and instruction."

To bridge the communications gap with P/Cs, here is a magic phrase that many have found to *convey* the understanding that is so necessary to effective communication. It is: "I know exactly how you feel. If I were in your shoes, I'd feel the same way . . ." Then pause just a moment.

The other person will physically and mentally relax; his "guard" comes down a little. He will be more receptive and ready to listen.

Simply stated, the principle is: *Concede*—before you *contend*.

Is this insincere? Not at all. If you really were the other person, if you *were* in his shoes, you *would* feel the way he does.

Try this phrase socially or professionally. You'll see how easy it is, how it will eliminate ill-feelings and create good will.

HOW THE P/C EVALUATES YOUR CASE PRESENTATION

At the two extremes of P/C evaluation of your case presentation are these two alternatives:

A) Where the benefits and value of proceeding with professional services outweigh the costs and obligations involved, or at the opposite extreme.

B) Where "procrastination" seems more appropriate and appealing than "action."

The relationship of these factors, as with most other aspects of professional practice, depends not so much on the facts per se, but what the P/C *thinks* the facts are. And it is the P/C who must make the *final* evaluation.

Of course, if the P/C is "captive," literally with no alternative or other choice at his or her disposal, then the P/C *must* act without further delay. The P/C in this case will "accept" anything, but possibly with misgivings and resentment.

If, on the other hand, the P/C does have an "elective choice," an alternative— whether to procrastinate or even "switch"—there is a strong possibility that he will exercise that option.

And in any event, there is *always* P/C "freedom of choice," if not for service, then for making referrals.

The objectives then, of a totally aligned case presentation, can be stated as:

1. To inform and motivate the P/C to a proper course of action.

2. To put costs and obligations involved in proper perspective.

Other than technical competence, these challenges are the essence of attaining a successful professional practice.

FIFTEEN TESTED IDEAS
FOR SUCCESSFUL CASE PRESENTATION

Here, in summary form from the preceding chapters, is a checklist for case presentation:

1. *attitude*—To inform and motivate the P/C to a proper course of action is more than the necessary connecting link between "discovering the problem"

and "solving the problem." It is a professional obligation and a disservice to the P/C if not properly done.

2. *environment*—The proper environment for the practitioner, as well as the P/C, creates a climate for communication, understanding and receptivity.

3. *empathy*—First, foremost and always we are in the "people business." Only *people* can say "yes," write checks and send referrals.

4. *inform*—Tell people the "complete story." *Inform*—before, during and after you *perform*.

5. *visual aids*—People learn 83 percent by *sight*, only 17 percent by all other senses combined. Use methods that tell *and* show.

6. *benefits*—Don't emphasize the service, but what the service *does* for the P/C, in terms meaningful to the P/C.

7. *limitations*—Be realistic about the P/C's obligations and the outcome.

8. *value*—Make "value received" greater than "fee paid" by explaining *what* is being done, *how* it is being done, both the obvious and the less obvious.

9. *future appointments*—Pave the way for preventive maintenance and periodic review by emphasizing the importance of "preventing" trouble rather than just "coping" with it.

10. *objections*—Encourage questions and uncover objections to make the P/C convinced, rather than confused. Engender P/C "acceptance," not "procrastination."

11. *assume*—Don't prejudge the P/C's ability, interest, and motivation to want the *best* in professional services. Give the P/C a chance to say "No."

12. *ask*—Don't wait for the P/C to take the initiative regarding services, fees, or preventive maintenance. Adopt a positive approach.

13. *ask "which"*—Give the P/C a "choice" between "something" and "something," not between "something" and "nothing." Make it easy for the P/C to say "yes" by suggesting *two* appointment times, *two* methods of payment, etc.

14. *keep statistics*—Keep track of case presentation results to determine the number of those who "follow through" and those who "procrastinate." Be *aware* of communication-breakdowns.

15. *change*—Try new methods, new verbal skills, and new ideas to improve P/C acceptance and practice growth.

WHEN A CASE PRESENTATION FIRST BEGINS

Is it when the P/C first walks into the office?

Is it when the P/C first telephones the office?

Contrary to common belief, a case presentation starts before either of these events, long before the P/C sees or hears you. It starts when the P/C first *hears* about you from an enthusiastic third party.

It's the referral in this case that paves the way for P/C acceptance—better than any case-presentation technique or any visual aid.

In fact, if the referral is enthusiastic enough, it may eliminate altogether the need for communication between "diagnosing" and "doing."

10

Fees—
Some Facts and Fallacies

"Man," it has been said, "is the only creature on earth who can talk himself into trouble."

After a couple of million years of practice, we've become pretty good at it.

Every day, in every walk of life, communication breakdowns occur; disagreements and frustrations arise; and, most of the time, it's because we did not really understand what someone else said, or they did not seem to understand what we really meant.

Life would be a lot simpler if things were just accepted at "face value." But it resists human nature to do so. We interpret and interpolate situations based on our background, experience and our perspectives.

Puzzle: Are the two inner circles of both groups in the diagram below equal, larger or smaller than each other?

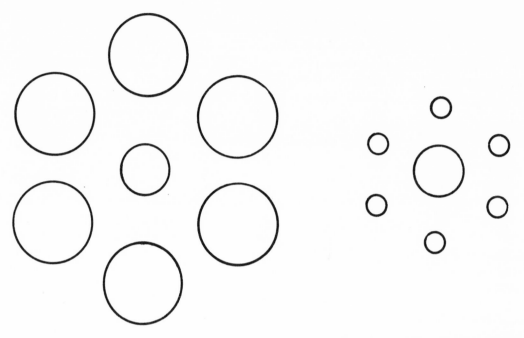

Solution: Although most people report the inner circle on the *right* appears larger, the fact is that both inner circles are equal in size. They appear to be unequal only because of the contrasting elements.

If we label the inner circles "professional fees" and the outer circles "P/C education," the puzzle of why the cost of professional services *seems* higher to some P/Cs is unraveled.

The relative value of *fees,* as in all other aspects of professional practice, depends on "communication."

HOW TO PREPARE BILLS
THAT MAKE DOLLARS AND SENSE

The fact that some P/Cs criticize and complain about the cost of professional services is no illusion. (Collection agencies have a thriving business because of it.) Part of the problem stems from a lack of communication as, for example, when a bill is rendered with the only notation being "for professional services."

There is no doubt about it. Standing by itself, without explanation or amplification, a long figure of $xx for complete professional services is, in fact, a wide open invitation to criticism. A preponderance of complaints of "over-charging" can be traced directly to the lone figure method of billing.

Fallacy: To many people, $45 a day for a hospital room represents only "room and board."

Fact: Hospital rates include a lot more than just "room and board." They include housekeeping, maintenance, and laundry services geared not only to the patient's comfort but also to guard against infection and injury. They include carefully prepared meals delivered to the bedside, plus special diets and nourishments as needed. They include use of routine supplies and equipment. They include careful recording of every detail of treatment and progress. And, of course, they include the biggest component— professional services (including nursing care) around the clock.

At some hospitals, professional services are being itemized separately, as follows:

1 day room and board @ $15 .... $15.00
1 day (24 hrs.) professional services @ $1.25 per hr. 30.00
                                                                   ————
                                                                   $45.00

The total charge is the same. But this simple itemization and explanation puts in better perspective the two thirds of a typical U.S. hospital's budget that is spent on labor costs—and seldom appreciated (or even known) by patients. Compared to costs on the "outside," both itemized charges appear reasonable, if not low. (In this case, the $1.25 per hour represents a pro-rated share of all labor costs including services of orderlies and nurses.)

Fallacy: To many people, $300 in lawyer's fees for incorporating a firm represents only such simple procedures as "filling out a form." On the surface, this seems exorbitant.

Fact: A detailed, itemized bill for legal services in connection with incorporation might look like this:

—Conferences with client and accountant with reference to corporation structure, preparing Articles of Incorporation and securing their execution, filing same to secure charter.

—Preparing bylaws and corporation record book, including minutes of incorporation meeting, first meeting of stockholders and first meeting of the Board of Directors.

—Preparing and issuing stock certificates ...... $300.

Fallacy: Veterinary clients who are billed $15 for having their dog's teeth cleaned cannot help but compare it with the charges from their dentist. It may, in some cases, be more than they pay themselves. Un-itemized billing in this instance does not present a favorable (or accurate) image of veterinary fees for this service.

Fact: Approximately $7 of the total charge is for the "anesthetic," which humans don't receive. Knowing this, does it change the "picture?"

What then are we really doing when we itemize a bill? We don't have to put ourselves in a P/C's shoes to understand this. We are already in them. We have all received bills for professional services. And we all know how it feels to receive a lump sum bill without a word of explanation.

And it is not so much what the itemization says as what the *lack* of it says.

The blank space around that lone lump sum figure says, loud and clear (take your pick):

"I don't care what you think."

"You may care about details but I'm too busy to bother."

"Money matters may be important to you but they're not to me."

"Take it or leave it."

"I've padded the bill and I don't want you to know how much."

On the other hand, itemization says just as loud and just as clear:

"I want you to understand the nature of this charge."

"I had to make the computations to arrive at a total. Here are the details."

"If you or your family have any questions about all or part of it, I'd be glad to provide further information."

"I consider your concern for expense as important as my own."

"This bill represents a reasonable charge for services rendered, as you can see."

Time after time, I have heard P/Cs complain of exorbitant fees and accuse their practitioners of "overcharging" for a service, while in the *same community* other P/Cs in the *same socio-economic bracket*, having received essentially the *same service* (or what they *think* is the same service) at the *same fee*, have spoken of *their* practitioners in glowing terms.

As in the case of the circle puzzle, it's not necessarily the size of the fee, but the size of the elements (information) that go with it.

ITEMIZE WHAT'S NOT BEING CHARGED, TOO

Practitioners often perform time-consuming services for P/Cs at "no charge" but fail to notify the P/C. The irony of this is that the uninformed P/C not only fails to appreciate these "extras" but can be the very one who later accuses the practitioner of overcharging.

One of the most obvious of these costly items is "consultation." Often there are *extended* consultations, either in the office or by phone, with members of the family or with an over-anxious P/C.

Other categories of "no charge" services may include an extra office visit, laboratory tests (or retests), special memoranda, reports, and countless other "behind the scenes" services including preparation, planning, inter- or intra-professional consultations, and *future services* (as in the case of contact lenses, hearing aids, and dentures).

Fallacy: Itemized bills may be appropriate for supermarkets and automobile repairs but they are out of place and unnecessary in the professional office.

Fact: People appreciate knowing for what they are being charged (or not being charged) regardless of the service or product purchased.

What the practitioner tends to take for granted as too "run of the mill" to mention is frequently information welcomed by the P/C—an "eye opener" as to the real value of the practitioner's services.

Suggestion: Don't convert your entire billing system first; but just try the idea, say for a week, especially with the *new* P/C. If the reaction is favorable, continue it, perhaps incorporating items on pre-printed slips which will simplify the system still further.*

Take a "telephone consultation" or, if you prefer, an "extended telephone consultation." The mere appearance of such an item on a fee slip "implies" that, on occasion, it can be a routine and ordinary charge. When it is then marked "n/c" (no charge), it psychologically enhances the value of this service while at the same time discourages, in a subtle way, unnecessary phone calls that disrupt office routine.

Another example: A prominent public speaker I know will include, on his statement of fees and expenses to a distant city, "2 days' travel time—no charge"—an item which is often overlooked by program chairmen.

"MY TIME IS YOUR TIME"

Many practitioners actually work fifty to sixty hours a week when you take into account "homework"—those additional hours devoted to study, research, and preparation on behalf of the P/C.

Yet, the P/C measures only that time he is a witness to. Unless he is advised, he has no reason to alter his erroneous time concept.

Some practitioners do this by sending information copies of letters sent on the P/C's behalf or brief memoranda summarizing steps taken or other efforts for the P/C.

Lawyers, for example, inform their clients with copies of briefs, pleadings, correspondence between counsels, memoranda of fact or law, depositions and written reports of all significant office conferences and hearings.

These don't say, "Look how much time I am spending on you. Be prepared for a large bill."

They really say, "I don't want you to be in the dark about what progress is being made; I want to keep you thoroughly informed."

In these days of low-cost photocopying, it's easy to keep P/Cs informed, and it's a cinch they'll appreciate it.

Question: Does a surgeon who charges $250 for an operation that takes thirty minutes have an equivalent income of $500 an hour? Here is an analysis:

Actual Time

Before Surgery:
Two 30-minute initial examinations
10 minutes, consultation with referring physician
15 minutes, study of x-rays
20 minutes on phone calling hospital admittance office and later talking with two members of the family—each of whom called inquiring about the patient.

---

* For further reading on the subject of pre-printed fee slips, see Chapters 10–11 of *The $100,000 Practice and How to Build It*, Prentice-Hall, Inc., Englewood Cliffs, New Jersey, 1966.

Two 15-minute visits including evaluation and interpretation of laboratory
tests before surgery

Surgery:

30 minutes for operation

25 minutes, checking final details, "scrubbing" and changing clothes

After Surgery:

45 minutes, conference with family, re-check in recovery room, writing up of
orders and changing clothes

Seven 15-minute visits during seven-day recuperation

50 minutes, consisting of 2 post-operative visits, filling out insurance forms
and writing a report to the referring physician.

Total time: 390 minutes—6½ hours.

And what about the considerably longer period of training (and subsequent
shorter years of productive practice), the demands of continuing education, the greater degree of risk and responsibility, etc?

Answer: Remember that it is not how much time you spend on a case, it is how
much time the P/C *thinks* you spend on it. There is no pat way to educate the P/C
on this total time factor. However, once you are convinced that the need for this education exists, the right time, the right place, and the right media will become evident
to you.

HOW TO QUOTE A FEE

How you say *what* you say, can be mighty important. It can change the entire
meaning and interpretation of whatever you're saying. Nowhere is this concept more
important than at the time of fee discussion.

How you verbally quote a fee can be as important as the fee itself. The tone of
your voice, your inflections, your manner, and above all your *attitude* about the fee,
can influence the P/C, for better or for worse.

A fee, regardless of the amount involved, quoted with timidity and hesitation (or
with what *sounds* like timidity and hesitation), is easily picked up by the P/C and
creates doubts and uncertainties where none would otherwise exist. It can, for example,
plant the seed of doubt that your fee is too high; it may even be construed as an invi-
tation to "bargain."

A fee, especially a *high* fee, quoted with complete indifference and disinterest can,
in effect, say "I couldn't care less" or "with your income, you can afford it." This needless interpretation can create resentment (as it might if implied about *you*).

Many professional people are squeamish about fee discussions. It's unpleasant,
uncomfortable and they frankly don't like it. Some try to avoid these discussions with
statements such as "You'll have to discuss that with the girl," or "We'll be as reasonable as we can," or "Let's not worry about that. Let's concentrate on getting you well
(out of trouble, etc.)."

This, if you'll pardon my saying, is asking for *T*rouble with a capital "T," especially if the practitioner has also avoided P/C education along the way. None but the most outspoken P/Cs will inquire further. The others will be inhibited or "frightened off." (Most P/Cs don't like fee discussions any more than practitioners do.)

When the bill does finally arrive, it may well come as a surprise, possibly for the worst. With the P/C now past the "crisis" and feeling a little less inhibited, the practitioner may end up being the one who is most surprised when the P/C complains about the fee, or refuses to pay the bill, or worse.

The alternative is to discuss fees in advance in an informative, down-to-earth way. Be natural. Be positive.

You might even be paid in advance.

SIX ADVANTAGES OF SCHEDULING MULTIPLE VISITS

Many practitioners schedule multiple visits for a given P/C, notwithstanding the fact that they could complete the consultation or examination with just one appointment. It might do to discuss this system here because there are fee implications. Certainly there are communications factors at work which bear scrutiny. These practitioners have cited the following advantages of multiple visits:

1) They provide the opportunity to give *complete* professional services including many "extras" that, although not absolutely essential, do nonetheless insure greater accuracy and thoroughness (i.e., the "ultimate" in quality care).

2) Due to such circumstances as emotional involvement and a host of other physical and/or psychological factors, the original symptoms (conditions, attitudes) may be exaggerated on the initial visit. A second appointment, in such cases, provides an opportunity for comparison and re-evaluation of the case. In many instances, it has been found that the problem has changed in direction or degree of severity.

3) If initial recommendations are not adequate, there is an opportunity to re-evaluate the case and suggest additional measures, insuring the chances that the case will be completed successfully.

4) A second appointment allays P/C's anxieties (or anger) if he fails to get the results he expected. It can, at times, eliminate belligerent feelings that could conceivably arise under such circumstances. At all times, it assures the P/C of the practitioner's continued interest and concern.

5) A second appointment provides still another opportunity for P/C education and motivation for *additional needed* services. These may have been recommended but not acepted on the first visit. This additional acceptance is not uncommon and may occur for three reasons: (a) A lessening of tension or anxiety as the P/C becomes more relaxed, more friendly and at ease and subsequently more cooperative; (b) The additional time has given the practitioner a chance to prepare a more complete, better organized, and more convincing case presentation than would be possible with just one visit; (c) Any improvements made as a result of initial recommendations will serve as an incentive for the P/C to consider additional services. Sometimes improve-

ments occur of which the P/C is not aware. A second appointment gives the practitioner the opportunity to bring these to the P/C's attention.

6) Studies have shown that P/Cs have a tendency to evaluate the fee in terms of the number of office visits. Two half-hour appointments, for example, appear to have more value than one full hour visit. This factor by itself would not, of course, justify inconveniencing the P/C for a second appointment but, combined with the distinct possibility of the other reasons metntioned, it does have its place in this discussion.

A Prentice-Hall Missouri Bar Association study was recently undertaken to determine the public's views as to the most important factors in setting charges for legal fees.

The following list of actual number of responses in each category is the result of that survey: *

Factor Mentioned	# Responses	% Total Responses
Effort expended by attorney	243	47%
Case involved (nature, complexity importance)	95	18
Ability to pay	82	15
Potential ability of lawyer (including experience, skill, staff)	31	6
Value received (success of result)	32	6

It is most interesting to note that "effort expended by the attorney" was mentioned *almost three times* as often as any other factor.

Aparently clients do not rate "success of results" as a leading factor in setting charges for legal fees. The obvious explanation of this rather surprising finding is, in fact, a credit to lawyers: Their clients appear to take for granted that the lawyer will get successful results, and do not consider winning or losing a case (except in contingency fee cases) a leading basis for setting the fee.

In this respect, we have found similar attitudes among patients (in the healing art professions) who regard effort as a significant factor in determining the fee *when a successful result is achieved.* However, when a *poor result* or *no result* is achieved, the patient is less apt to recognize the time and effort expended by the practitioner and therefore less willing to accept an equivalent fee.

Interestingly enough, many practitioners look upon success of results as a dominant factor in setting fees, with ability and skill running a close second place. Such views are obviously in sharp contrast with those of P/Cs. They point up the extent of the "communications gap" and difference of attitudes and perspectives that so frequently exist between practitioner and P/Cs.

So, to whatever extent multiple visits suggest "extra effort," it might be valuable to the practitioner to consider, when appropriate, the "split appointment."

To be sure, scheduling multiple appointments should not be done to merely "impress" the P/C. And in any event, such appointment scheduling should not be a hard and fast rule. The prudence of such a policy depends on many factors. It most

* *Lawyers Practice Manual* (Prentice-Hall, Englewood Cliffs, N.J., 1964).

certainly merits the consideration of those practitioners wishing to adjust their practice in a quality-oriented direction.

IS YOUR PROFESSIONAL IMAGE UP TO DATE?

For many years, doctors have insisted that fees are based on time, skill and knowledge, that these are the main ingredients of their professional services. (Lawyers have emphasized that time and advice are their "stock in trade.") The public has accepted this. But now this boon to P/C billing is proving to be a boomerang.

Computers, electronic data processing, and high speed equipment have greatly reduced the time factor in many professional services.

Should fees be reduced?

Yes, says the public.

But in saying yes, the public is unaware of the investment needed to acquire this equipment, the costs to maintain and house it, and the additional training and costs to operate it.

In the surveys that we take of public opinion concerning professional services (Chapter 12), one of the questions is: "How much investment would you estimate (guess) your [specialist] has in office equipment and professional facilities?" (followed by three ranges of cost, the figure depending on the professional specialty).

In the veterinary field, for example, the usual estimate is in the $10,000–$25,000 range.

The facts are that including the land and the building—which most veterinarians own—the investment range is closer to $75,000–$100,000!

That's quite a communications gap.

As a result, many veterinarians take new clients on a brief tour of their facilities, introducing them to members of their staff, and pointing out special features such as examining and surgery areas, laboratory and diagnostic equipment, and hospitalization areas, including "intensive care" sections.

To the uninitiated client, it is invariably a revelation. Most admit they never realized a veterinary hospital could be so complete.

And these few minutes invested in client education make a complete difference in attitude and appreciation when the bill arrives. More than that, these efforts pay big dividends in the clients' peace of mind, knowing their pets are getting the best in modern, veterinary medical attention.

The gap between "cost-conscious" P/Cs and "service-conscious" P/Cs exists in many professions only because they have never been told differently.

Much has been said and written about the "high cost of dying"; yet few people realize that a complete funeral service includes fifty or more services, that these services are available twenty-four hours a day, seven days a week, and that they represent seventy or more man hours of professional time.

The emphasis in too many cases has been placed on the funeral ceremony itself, which is only a small part of the total service, and on the funeral merchandise. Ignored are the many personal services performed by the members of this profession and the substantial investment in capital needed to house and perform them.

To help fill the knowledge void among his patients, a midwest dentist sets aside a few minutes of the new patient's first visit to explain the procedures in his office, which he adds "may be a little different than those of your last dentist."

This orientation includes a brief explanation of his high-speed equipment, panoramic x-ray unit, and "four-handed" dental procedures. He does this in terms meaning-than with old-fashioned methods.

And these few minutes mean that his patients have a higher dental I.Q. regarding his professional services, his equipment, and his fees.

In the field of dentistry, as in all professions, the era of technological breakthrough is just beginning. In a recent article appearing in *Business Week,* it was reported that dental research is on the threshold of a series of developments that will change the whole look of dentistry. During the next decade, it was predicted among other things that: "Time in the dentist's chair will be sliced in half. There will be no waiting for bridges; instead, plastic implants, carbon copies of the original teeth, will be inserted within minutes after the original teeth are removed." *

It's easy to see that even *today's* professional image will be fast going out of date. The challenge of keeping oneself and one's P/Cs up to date will require, as the Red Queen said to Alice: ". . . all the running you can do, to keep in the same place." **

INFORM—DON'T IMPRESS

In bringing P/Cs up to date on professional services, facilities and fees, be careful not to let an intent to *inform* become an attempt to *impress* the P/C.

The first is educational, motivational and helpful to the P/C in terms of understanding the benefits and value of complete professional services. In a quality practice, it is an integral part of the *complete* case presentation.

On the other hand, when it is an attempt to *impress* the P/C, it becomes false, put-on and is quickly seen through.

The difference is slight but vital—frequently more a matter of degree than kind. It depends on the underlying motive (or what the P/C *thinks* is the underlying motive).

In the presence of one who informs and explains, the P/C is interested and appreciative. When confronted with a practitioner who tries to impress and overwhelm, the P/C is uncomfortable and starts looking for the nearest exit, mentally if not physically.

The alternative can be almost as bad. The practitioner should not shrug off his ability or accomplishments with misplaced modesty. To reply to a P/C who compliments his work or thanks him for the results achieved with a casual "it's routine procedure" or "think nothing of it," is belittling.

It may backfire when the P/C sees the bill.

---

* "Dentistry's Brave New World," *Business Week,* May 2, 1968, reprinted by permission.
** From *Through the Looking Glass* by Lewis Carroll.

It is not boasting or bragging to tell the P/C the "complete story" of the technical equipment behind a bill or the "behind the scenes" efforts to help him. If told in a matter-of-fact, informative way, it acts the same as itemizing a bill. It shows the P/C that you are interested in communicating with him.

One day, with more of the complete picture in mind, people will stop multiplying the fee by the hours, times eight hours a day, times six days a week, times fifty-two weeks a year, and arriving at a grossly exaggerated and inflated income.

Fee disputes will lessen. And more P/Cs will be heard expressing the ultimate in acceptance: "Is that all you are charging?"

They might even send you an apple pie.

11

How to Prevent
Practice Drop-Outs

A Florida surgeon recently reported that it was necessary to return more patients to the operating room after surgery during times when there was a full moon. Looking into this further, he found that almost all attacks of bleeding ulcers occurred when the moon was full.

Man's health and life are tied in with his emotions. This is dramatically demonstrated by the way crimes of passion, murders, and arson increase with the full moon. Research at Duke University has shown that even such emotions as apathy, pent-up hostility, or amiability and well-being, rise and fall with the phases of the moon.

Even *what* your P/Cs think of you can fluctuate with the moon. You can't please all of your P/Cs all of the time, but you can come closer if you aim for their emotions.

Within the past twenty-five years, a client-oriented point of view in psychotherapy has received much attention. With Dr. Carl R. Rogers as one of its prime movers, the concept is based on the idea that the therapist is a "genuine," real person struggling to achieve an accurate empathy for the patient based on a positive regard for him. The therapist is his "actual self," during encounters with the patient, when expressing his own feelings and attitudes without facade. As Dr. Rogers describes it, the therapist meets the patient "person to person, being himself, not denying himself."

And down go a few more Ivory Tower Attitudes.

It is not easy for a person to share his feelings with another person and truly be himself. But if a practitioner can succeed at least part of the way, he can create lifetime friends with many P/Cs and certainly reduce the attrition to which every practice is subject.

HOW TO SEE YOUR PRACTICE
IN PSYCHOLOGICAL PERSPECTIVE

Often the ability to identify with and attract P/Cs is unconscious and not even noticed by practitioners.

Case History: I recently conferred with a New York City practitioner who maintained two offices, one in a prestige, midtown New York office building and a second in his suburban home town. The latter was a community of young, middle-income families. Notwithstanding the volume of high-income business executives in his midtown office, his suburban practice was more successful.

After some discussion, he revealed that his midtown clients were quite rich, successful and famous. In fact, three of them had appeared on the cover of *Time* Magazine. He admitted that they tended to awe him, even frighten him at times. He simply was not as "comfortable" in their presence as he was with his home town clients with whom he found it easier to talk and be with.

The tendency to identify with and relate to certain types of P/Cs is natural and, to a large extent, unavoidable. For instance, I've met many younger practitioners who tend to identify and communicate best with the specific P/C groups that I have heard some psychologists refer to as the "Y.A.V.I.S." type (*young—attractive—verbal—intelligent—successful*). They are more at ease with these P/Cs and seem to be able to do more for them.

If a practitioner has these "leanings" toward certain types of P/Cs, he should be aware of them. If the practitioner cannot be comfortable and at ease with his P/Cs, it is bound to affect P/C communication and "drop-outs."

The reverse is also true. If P/Cs have difficulty identifying with the practitioner, if they are in awe of *him*, they too will be uncomfortable and ill at ease in his presence —hesitant to confide, afraid to ask questions, etc. This is why it is so important for a practitioner to "humanize" his relationships with P/Cs, environmentally and psychologically.

Here is a simple but revealing way to see your practice and your P/Cs in truer psychological perspective. Select fifty P/C names at random from the files. Alongside each name, decide if you would like to meet these people socially, whether you really "like" them, and are comfortable with them. Are there some (many) that you don't like, who annoy you and whom you would just as soon never see again?

Do the negatives outnumber the positives? If so, and if your practice is not as successful as you'd like it to be or think it should be, this lack of rapport could be a contributing cause—if not *the* cause—of practice attrition.

HOW TO DEVELOP RAPPORT WITH P/Cs

The key to a P/C-centered practice is a high regard for the P/C. Some day, somebody will write a book singing a song of people. People are really wonderful, and the practitioners who haven't discovered this yet are in for a thrilling surprise.

The trouble is many P/Cs come in with two masks on. One they wear for your benefit, hiding their fears and worries, their self-recognized weaknesses and eccentricities; the other they wear for their own benefit, closing off those other traits from their consciousness which they refuse to acknowledge in themselves.

And what about the practitioner? Is he totally maskless?

Here, we have two people "facing" each other, both of whom want to be liked by the other, but who may never see each other's true self. You cannot expect a mutual high regard to spring up between two masked figures.

Recently, an editorial in the *Bulletin* of the Bergen County Medical Society in New Jersey commented: "We live in an age of image building, an age where the mask is more important than the face behind it. The image we are talking about is that of the efficient, never wrong, scientific superbeing. People never thought of suing the friendly, often bumbling, always human doctors they used to know. But, when faced with the new image of impersonal machines for curing, they take great delight in slapping us down." *

You, as a professional, cannot remove the other fellow's mask. But you can start the de-masking process in two ways:

1) Drop you own mask. Be natural. Try to make him a friend as well as a P/C.
2) Look through his mask. See him as a person, not a P/C. Look past the problems and see the other person who has brought the problems to you.

This is the essence of a humanized practice.

Pretty soon, as you become aware of your own feelings toward the P/C and learn his feelings toward you, you the practitioner become more at home in the world of your client.

This is the beginning of rapport. And rapport is a two-way street.

This rapport works miracles. We are considering practice success in terms of extra-technical dimensions, but rapport makes itself felt even in the effectiveness of method and technique. It permeates the atmosphere with confidence and expectation.

This rapport does not come as easily between the practitioner and the P/C as it does between two people sitting in a living room. The people in the living room seek and expect rapport. The P/C is with you because he is in trouble. He is forced by human nature, health, the law, or outside events into a situation he has not wanted or

---

* Dr. Albert D. Carilli: *Bulletin* of the Bergen County Medical Society (February, 1966).

sought. It is costing time, money and effort. He is bitter, even resentful. He is not reaching consciously for rapport. He may be looking for a scapegoat to strike back at, or he may simply be inhibited.

Many P/Cs are afraid to take the lead in establishing rapport. They reason that it's not their place to do so. They are, in a sense, the "uninvited guest" in a professional office. They may fear doing or saying the wrong thing, or their natural shyness may compel them to be withdrawn and taciturn. Not being sure of the "right" things to do, they play it safe by doing nothing.

That's why the first ten seconds, the first ten words, can be so important in setting the stage for communication.

The antidote? Shed your "front." Be your understanding, "living room" self. Feel concern, empathy, love.

Take the initiative. It can be a smile, a handshake or a kind word. Say something complimentary at this point, and you may even turn a lemon into a lemonade!

Permit your warm, human side to show and you melt the ice. A stranger becomes a friend.

R. A. Whitney, T. Rubin, and J. D. Murphy, authors of *The New Psychology of Persuasion and Motivation in Selling,** cite numerous experiments by behavioral scientists proving that, in making judgments of others, you "see" what you "look for." "If we're *looking* for a friendly, warm, sincere person, the chances are good we will see much evidence of it; but, if we start out expecting the other person to be unfriendly, hostile, etc., the chances are also very good that we will find plenty of evidence to support this view too."

They point out that a great many people get themselves into trouble because of their "expectations" that the other person will resist. It is curious but true, they say, that the man who approaches other people, with the conviction that they are going to resist with blind stubbornness any idea he presents, will in all probability find them responding in just that way. "The process is clear: whenever he treats the people who are supposed to buy his ideas as if they were bullheaded, he changes the way they are used to being treated, and they *will* be bullheaded in resisting that change."

To a large degree the practitioner has it within his power to determine his P/C's receptivity, cooperation and enthusiasm. By his own attitude and pre-conceived judgments of the P/C and by his own behavior, he exerts a powerful influence over the P/C.

But to make it work, you must go to work on your own attitudes and basic beliefs about other people rather than trying to force the attitudes of others directly. Change your own approach, and the other person's receptivity changes by a sort of reflex action. So why not take the first step? Just assume from the outset that the P/C is basically receptive, cooperative, friendly and that he means well, regardless of his "mask." You'll be correct in your assumption 85 percent of the time. But, if you begin with the assumption that the other person is going to be uncooperative and hard to get along with, you'll be correct almost 100 percent of the time.

As friendship ripens, you may be far from liking the P/C as you would a buddy, but it is enough to change the polarity, to set the stage for two-way communication on a more meaningful level. The P/C feels this change and "warms up."

---

* Whitney, Rubin, and Murphy, *The New Psychology of Persuasion and Motivation in Selling* (Prentice-Hall, Inc., Englewood Cliffs, N.J., 1965).

Even animals react differently when handled by people who feel affection for them, as any pet owner knows. Speaking on this subject at a recent meeting of the Canadian Association for Research in Toxicology, Dr. Eldon Boyd, Professor of Pharmacology at Queen's University, Kingston, Ontario, spoke of one technician who liked the rats being used in certain experiments and even gave them names. When she went to their cages to give them drugs, which was done by a stomach tube in their mouths, the rats ran to her and offered little or no resistance—even though a stomach tube for them is no joy.

Pointing out that similar results could be found in people, he suggested that doctors take the emotional factor into account when dealing with patients.

THE PRACTICE-BUILDING FACTS OF LIFE

Every practice has its share of drop-outs. People lose interest and their initial motivation wanes with the passage of time. The forces pulling them exceed the forces pushing them.

Then there are the acute or extreme cases who abruptly stop or switch to another practitioner.

Rapport is not the whole answer. Without it, nothing else will help. But with it, the stage is set for a meaningful and lasting relationship.

In a setting of rapport, the P/C is receptive to know everything about his problem that you know. He listens to a case presentation with attentiveness and concentration. His pores are open.

If a P/C knew and understood what you knew and understood about his problem, if he comprehended what could and should be done about it and the value of preventive maintenance, then:

—You would have complete and enthusiastic acceptance, cooperation and implementation of all recommendations.

—There would be virtually no resistance to fees, time involved or any other "inconveniences."

—There would be no drop-outs, and every case would be completed and maintained successfully.

But P/Cs don't always know what they should know. Because of fear, apathy, or ignorance, some say "no." And they can say "no" in many ways: "I want to think it over." "I want another opinion." "I'll call you when I return from vacation." And they continue to procrastinate.

HOW TO PREVENT ONE DROP-OUT
FROM LEADING TO ANOTHER

In Chapter 3, we said that if you were to plot a graph of a growing practice—one that was reacting to a humanizing program—the result would be an upward curve rather than an upward straight line. It was pointed out that once growth starts, it begins to accelerate at a faster and faster rate.

To some extent, the reverse deceleration process is similar, since one drop-out leads to another. It has a tendency to gather momentum, not so much because of one P/C influencing another, but because of the effect it can have on the practitioner himself.

The Ivory Tower Attitude may have permitted some practitioners to consider themselves immune from personal problems. The fact is, practitioners have as many emotional needs as their P/Cs. In fact, they are P/Cs themselves—physicians go to attorneys, accountants, to dentists, and vice versa, in a perpetual "la ronde."

A recent article in *Redbook* (November, 1968) caused a small furor in the medical profession when it asserted that "most doctors can't help women with sex problems." It quoted members of the medical profession criticizing the limited education that medical students receive in counseling on such matters. As a result, they said, many medical graduates are frequently naive, may have sexual problems of their own, and may ignore sexual and emotional causes of physical symptoms.*

Perhaps I am reaching too far for proof positive that practitioners have their own emotions. At any rate, it is their own human response to, or rather their definition of "drop-out" that can set the stage for another drop-out.

In some practitioners' minds, P/C "procrastination" is a form of drop-out. So is the unappreciative P/C for whom he has rendered a valuable service. Some extend the definition so far as to include the P/C who won't pay a bill or send a referral.

Many consider these unappreciative or uncooperative acts as a personal rejection. They exaggerate the significance of these events beyond their importance and feel a dire need to be "loved," "approved," or "accepted" by every P/C for every service rendered.

When a "drop-out" does occur, these practitioners expose their "bruised" egos to other P/Cs who, in turn, sense this frustration, ennui and perhaps faltering confidence.

The "cure" for this is to accept the occasional dissatisfied, unappreciative, or uncooperative P/C as inevitable and the occasional drop-out as unavoidable, and go on to serve other P/Cs personally and professionally. Occasional drop-outs are a necessary weeding-out process and act to move a practice in the direction of being quality-oriented.

It was journalist Herbert Bayard Swope who wisely said: "I cannot tell you the formula for success, but I can tell you the formula for failure; try to please everyone."

It just can't be done.

PRACTICAL GOALS VERSUS
PERFECTIONISTIC GOALS

For some practitioners, a successful practice isn't quite enough. In spite of their achievements and accomplishments; in spite of an abundance of grateful, appreciative and enthusiastic P/Cs whose lives, health and welfare have been helped by their skills and knowledge; in spite of their enviable prestige among P/Cs and colleagues alike;

---

* *Redbook,* November, 1968. Copyright © 1968 by McCall Corporation.

and in spite of substantial practice income, these men feel frustrated and at times dismayed by the small percentage of P/Cs who—primarily because of their own hang-ups and neurotic needs—don't "turn on" for the practitioner, and ultimately "turn off" and "drop out."

These practitioners, despite sincere intentions, have unfortunately set perfection-istic goals rather than practical ones. For them, "hitting the bulls-eye" isn't enough. They have to hit "dead center" all the time.

It just can't be done.

Suggestions:

1. Don't try to be approved of and accepted by all P/Cs at all times. Adopt a "what will be will be" attitude—less perfectionistic, more permissive and philosophical.

2. Acknowledge to yourself the fact that some P/Cs, because of their own limita-tions, cannot accept advice and cannot give approval. It matters little that it is for their own benefit. This disapproval of a practitioner may be for reasons entirely beyond the practitioner's control ("He has brown eyes," for example).

3. Accept and approve yourself. When a practitioner is over-concerned with being approved and accepted by P/Cs, he begins to worry about "how much" and "how long." He wonders why the P/C doesn't send referrals and isn't more grateful and appreciative. It's an endless cycle that can best be broken by a total upgrading of his own self-esteem.

4. Take your desire to be approved and appreciated by P/Cs and shift it around, to be always approving and appreciative of P/Cs yourself.

5. Give up trying to win approval and be yourself. Ironically, the harder one tries to win approval, the more one loses ground. It can backfire. People lose respect for the practitioner. His motives become suspect. To some P/Cs it can be irritating, annoying, even boring.

Epictetus, the famous Stoic, in the first century A.D., wrote in *The Enchiridion* that "men are disturbed not by things, but by the views which they take of them."

Shakespeare, centuries later, rephrased this thought in *Hamlet*: "There's nothing either good or bad—but thinking makes it so."

P/Cs who switch, "telephone shoppers," "no-shows," "procrastinators," "do-it-yourselfers," and "deadbeats," all are part and parcel of every practice. To some extent they can be minimized. They can certainly be weeded out. But they cannot be elim-inated altogether.

For your own peace of mind, don't let them dominate your thinking. Don't let them influence your attitudes. Don't let them alter your policies. Remember, 90 percent of the frustrations, aggravations and annoyances in practice are caused by 10 percent of the P/Cs. So just let them go.

UNAVOIDABLE DROP-OUTS
AND HOW TO HANDLE THEM

Almost 40 million persons—close to one out of five in the population—move each year, according to the Census Bureau. About two out of three movers stay close to their previous surroundings, but the 13 million others move longer distances or across state lines.

This population movement year after year has tremendous significance for the professional practitioner, not only in terms of "drop-outs" and the need to replace them, but also in terms of the advantages of having intra-professional contacts throughout the country. Being able to send a P/C to a *known* colleague is an advantage to everyone.

A practitioner in Indiana makes it a policy to look up and compliment a speaker he has heard at a local, state or national meeting. Upon his return home, he will send him a note saying again how much he enjoyed the presentation, perhaps indicating how a particular idea has already been of value. He will do the same thing with authors of articles appearing in professional journals, perhaps "swapping" ideas with them.

These little notes sent in genuine appreciation have, as a bonus, broadened his professional contacts throughout the country. On occasions these friendships have resulted in out-of-town referrals in both directions.

When P/Cs tell you they will be moving away from your practice area, send them, if possible, a covering letter with the name of a practitioner in your specialty and known to you in the city to which they will be moving. Send a copy to the referred practitioner, adding a personal reference that will make the "get acquainted" process even easier.

This extra effort assures the P/C of immediate attention, if needed in the new city, and further evidences your continuing interest.

THE "DROP-OUT" REFERRAL RATIO

Statistics concerning drop-outs (other than those who die or move away) can be very informative, especially when combined with statistics on incoming referrals. They can provide valuable clues, over a period of time, to the direction and growth (or decline) of a practice.

For instance, high referrals, combined with a high drop-out rate in a field where continued maintenance, recall and/or review is the rule, indicate good professional and personal service (high referrals), but poor P/C education and motivation (high drop-outs).

Low referrals combined with low drop-outs indicate good professional service that keeps P/Cs satisfied, but apparently little *personal* service and "extras" that would make them enthusiastic enough to make referrals.

High referrals, low drop-outs is the ideal situation for most types of successful practices, while the opposite—low referrals, high drop-outs—spells trouble.

These statistics, if kept accurately, can provide you with advance warning of problems or, when encouraging, can lift you to new levels of personal gratification and enthusiasm.

12

How to Monitor Your Practice with Feedback

An Ohio dentist wrote me recently: "Practice growth, it seems, is a continuous uphill climb. The hang-ups that occur, which though very small, add up and become a weight and push you down. Hearing you at the Cleveland Dental Society meeting last month resulted in an adjustment of my altitude. Thank you for providing the fuel for the climb. The view is better from here."

We have talked of "attitude adjustment, " but "altitude adjustment" might be a better way to look at it. "Routine" clouds the perspective. It can bog us down unconsciously.

Then how do we know when we are down, and how do we make a change for the better—and higher?

The process of change can begin when a practitioner first recognizes that his practice has not reached its fullest potential of service and growth. Dissatisfaction replaces complacency when he admits there must be a better way of doing things. This, in turn, becomes *discontent* as he looks with receptivity for new ideas. Dissatisfaction and discontent lead to a *determination to change*. The results are almost immediate as change produces *improvements, enthusiasm* and a *higher level* of practice success.

The starting point is *recognition*; the turning point is *change*.

The uphill climb that leads to change takes motivation. This book may motivate. A seminar may motivate. But there is a more high-powered and immediate method in your office waiting to be tapped.

Your own P/Cs can provide the perspective so necessary to recognize the need for change. The key is "feedback."

HOW P/C FEEDBACK WORKS

I first discovered the feedback principle in the fascinating book *Cybernetics*, by Dr. Norbert Wiener. Cybernetics is a word coined by Dr. Wiener for the science of the automatic control of behavior. The book carries the interesting subtitle "Control and Communication in the Animal and the Machine."

Dr. Wiener speaks of the behavior of human beings and machines in the same context. Everything, he says, is full of parallels and surprising applications. The feedback principle, he explains, governs practically everything that human beings do, as well as everything that automatic machines do. He says: "The feedback principle means that behavior is scanned for its result and the success or failure of this result modifies future behavior."

Let's take two examples, one representing human reactions, the other that of an automatic machine. The simple act of picking up a pencil requires a multiplicity of actions and reactions. Your eyes locate the pencil, your brain issues the necessary commands to your nervous system, and you stretch your hand. As your hand approaches the pencil, your eyes register that fact and report back to the brain. Information, in this sense, is *fed back*. On the basis of that feedback, your brain issues revised commands to your nervous system and the muscles of your arm and hand and fingers—until finally, at the precise moment, your fingers are directed to grasp it. Feedback makes it possible for you to behave in such a way as to accomplish your purpose.

The most widely known and used automatic mechanism is a thermostat. The furnace in the basement heats the home. The thermostat in the living room registers the temperatures. When the room temperature reaches a certain pre-determined level, the thermostat feeds that information back to the furnace, which automatically shuts it off.

Psychological feedback works on the same principle, but by its very nature is more subtle, more difficult to evaluate. The trouble is that we don't have a thermostat to measure the "temperature" of P/Cs. If we knew, for example, the little things that caused some P/Cs to become "cold" and "turned off," small changes might be all that would be needed to prevent drop-outs, switching and needless procrastination. Conversely, if we could pin-point those factors that resulted in P/C enthusiasm, extra efforts could be applied with *all* P/Cs to improve rapport and referrals.

There are several alternatives to discover these valuable clues—through feedback.

THE PUBLIC OPINION SURVEY

A "full" appointment book and a minimum of P/C complaints has lulled many a practitioner into a sense of complacency that all is going well. Using these barometers of public opinion, practitioners have assumed they have excellent rapport with P/Cs.

Yet attitude surveys, conducted by my firm and others, have shown that many P/Cs do not share this opinion. Forced to seek professional services, trapped by a situation over which they have no control, many feel more "captive" than "captivated." Specific comments from these P/Cs have been included in preceding chapters; more will be mentioned in this one.

The following is an excerpt from one type of questionnaire we have used to obtain these comments in order to pin-point those aspects of professional services, attitudes and policies most in need of change. The questions have been reworded, in this case, to give them broader application for readers in varied fields.

As an interesting experiment, read through these questions as a *patient* (or *client*) of your own dentist (or physician, lawyer, or accountant etc.). To increase your objectivity, select the field *least familiar* to you.

Your reactions to the shortcomings or "I Care Attitudes" of *other* practitioners may provide valuable clues to the changes needed in your own practice.

1) How many years of college training do you think are required for licensure in the (specialty) profession?

4 years _____ 6 years _____ 8 years or more _____

2) How many hours per year would you estimate your [specialist] spends in formal, post-graduate courses related to his field?

none _____ 25 hours _____ 50 hours _____ 100 hours or more _____

3) How much investment would you estimate (guess) your [specialist] has in office equipment and professional facilities? (followed by three ranges of investment costs, the figures depending on the professional specialty—e.g.)

less than $5,000 _____ $5,000–$10,000 _____ $10,000–$20,000 _____

Comment: The answers to questions 1, 2 and 3 vary of course from one profession to another, let alone from one practice to another. Specific examples illustrating the extent of the professional communications gap have been cited in Chapters 5, 7 and 10. As a rule, most P/Cs underestimate the facts in all three cases.

Question: Was *your* background knowledge of other fields helped by educational brochures, bulletin board information, guided "tours" or practitioner explanations? Could these ideas be put to use in your practice?

4) How did you happen to go to your present [specialist]?

Friend's recommendation _____ knew him personally _____ telephone book _____ convenient location _____ read an article by (or about) him _____ heard him speak _____

Comment: Surveys show that the largest percentage of P/Cs select a practitioner on the basis of a referral, personal acquaintanceship, or a "reputation" established by an out-of-office activity. The basis of *your* selection of practitioners may provide additional insight as to the relative importance of "referrals" and "location."

5) How do you feel about the explanations and information your [specialist] provides about:

the details of the vist _____, fees _____, office policies (appointments, payments, office hours, insurance benefits, etc.) _____, follow-up instructions _____.

6) Does your [specialist] have a reminder system to notify you when you are due for a periodic examination (review)? _____ Do you (would you) appreciate such a system? _____

7) How would you rate your [specialist's]:

	very good	good	average	poor	don't know
Appointment system (promptness and availability)					
Reception room (comfort and conveniences)					
Professional assistants (courtesy and competence)					
Professional equipment and facilities					
Office in general					
Personal mannerisms					

Question: Would any of the Potlatch suggestions in Chapters 5 and 6 be appreciated?

8) Check which of the following services your [specialist] offers (followed by a list of complete professional services, including many important but less obvious services offered by the "above average" practitioner):

Note: Unfortunately, space does not permit us to reproduce here the variations for all professions. However, in Chapter 7 the "range of services" offered by Optometrists and Consulting Engineers were described in detail.

Comment: The purpose of this checklist is to determine the P/C's "Service I.Q." Most are aware of only "basic services," routine procedures, or those which they have personally received. The problem arises when P/Cs go elsewhere for a service their regular practitioner is qualified to perform, or worse —ignore the problem completely because of inadequate information.

9) What do you like best about your present [specialist]? _____

_____

10) What do you like least about your present [specialist]? _____

_____

Comment: The answers to questions 9 and 10 invariably show a greater concern with "human relations" than with "technical competence"—which most P/Cs seem to take for granted.

POINTS TO PONDER

We find the results of these surveys vary from one end of the altimeter to the other—from very limited "Service I.Q.s" and low opinions of practitioners to very high. It is always gratifying to get a predominance of positive reactions from a survey. But, since these surveys are aimed at improvement, it is the negative feedback that gets the spotlight and the corrective attention.

Here, for example, are some negative comments about practitioners in varying specialties as culled from these public opinion surveys:
1. Don't care about people's feelings or personal comfort.
2. Too impressed with their own importance.
3. Act as though they know everything.
4. Cold, distant, often patronizing.
5. Extra charges without warning or explanations.
6. Undue waiting, notwithstanding appointment.
7. Don't give enough information or explanation.
8. Abrupt, rude, and rushed.

Do such problems exist in your practice? Possibly not, but the fact that you have never heard "complaints" does not necessarily mean they don't exist. This is so simply because disgruntled P/Cs do not usually air their gripes with their practitioners. They may tell their friends or neighbors, or the hairdresser, or their business associates, but not a word gets to the one person who could work out a solution. So the problems continue, taking their toll in diminished practice growth. It is a vicious circle but not an unbreakable one. The first step must be taken by the practitioner.

HOW TO CONVERT NEGATIVE FEEDBACK
INTO PRACTICE GROWTH

Negative feedback from opinion surveys often has the effect of applying to everybody but the reader, or to be discounted or glossed over for some other reason.

We all have a tendency to react defensively to life's situations. It stems from a feeling that we are the target.

But practitioners are not the target of these public opinion surveys. Rather they are the beneficiaries. They have the ability to take this negative feedback and turn it into positive results.

If negative feedback is seen as a valuable identification of those areas where change is feasible, then a minimum effort will produce a decided improvement in public understanding and practice growth.

Further analysis of these surveys reveals that much of the negative feedback derives not so much from what the practitioner *does*, but from what he does *not* do. It is the "sin of omission," especially in the area of human relations, about which P/Cs are most vocal.

To convert negative feedback into practice growth means to take corrective action aimed at supplying the missing ingredients that the survey has uncovered.

These ingredients are what this book has been all about:

- A humanized dimension to demonstrate concern and understanding
- Improved communications to inform—before, during and after you perform.

HOW TO TAKE THE PULSE OF YOUR PRACTICE

The best insight occurs when you do your own survey. Here the negative feedback is even harder to transform from personal to objective status. But the effort is worth it because of the valuable direct information it provides on *your* services, *your* fees, and *your* policies.

Here is a typical survey that you can conduct. P/Cs appreciate your interest in their opinion. You should give the survey form to them in person; *Do not mail it.* Give them a postage-paid reply envelope and remind them that they have the option of returning it anonymously:

May we ask a few minutes of your time to answer these questions. They are intended to help us to be more considerate of your time and feelings. Thank you.

1. Did you receive the courteous attention you were led to expect from us by the friend who referred you? _____

    Comments: _____
2. Did we tell you enough about the problem that prompted your visit? _____ too much? _____
    Comments: _____
3. Were all procedures and fees adequately explained? _____
    Is there any further information desired? _____
    Comments: _____
4. What suggestions do you have to help us better serve you before, after, or even during the office visit? _____

Thank you for your assistance.

In health-care professions where "physical contact" is a factor, a question of added feedback value is: Were you treated gently? _____

A question of this type is of utmost importance, especially to the busy practitioner who may unintentionally, be "rougher" with patients than he thinks. Without feedback, verbal or otherwise, he will have no way of knowing, especially with the stoic patient.

In any event, don't underestimate the "public relations" value of asking your P/Cs' candid opinion of your service. It proves your concern for their feelings. The mere fact that you are interested may be more than they expected or received from other practitioners. It most certainly will be appreciated.

Is it "looking for trouble" to distribute such a questionnaire? No more so than recommending that P/Cs have an annual "review" or "examination" even though they have no "complaints" as such. Its purpose is to *prevent* trouble or at least, to catch it in the earliest possible stages. (The alternative, and it applies to all forms of feedback, is shown in the picture entitled "Food for Thought" shown at the end of Chapter 8.)

Hotels, airlines, restuarants and many other firms in the "people business" today recognize the value of feedback from their customers. Postage-paid forms are offered at check-out counters that invite the public's comments, suggestions and criticisms and invariably these forms are pre-addressed to the *presidents* of these firms. Many I have met, have told me it's the most important mail they receive and, on more than one occasion, it has resulted in a change of policy or procedure.

As a start, distribute a questionnaire of this type to 50 P/Cs. See what reaction you get. Going by the experience of those who have done it, you can expect an average return of 30–40 percent.

Be prepared for some surprises, both good and bad. Many replies will undoubtedly have some very flattering comments and praise. This positive feedback is also very valuable for it reassures you that you are indeed doing your best and your P/Cs are pleased.

And that's a nice feeling.

ANOTHER SOURCE OF VALUABLE FEEDBACK

Another way of "taking the pulse" of your practice from an entirely different perspective is to survey your *staff*. From the sidelines, they are in a position to see things that you, in an effort to maintain a busy schedule, might miss. As a liaison between you and the P/C, their relationship with the P/C and their "view" is different. As women, their "powers of intuition" should not be underestimated.

For many practitioners, staff feedback has been the key to practice growth.

Here is a questionnaire developed by H.P. Jacobi, DDS of Neenah, Wisconsin, from his excellent text *A Dentist's Flight Manual to Success.**

Dear Staff,

In our constant effort to keep the office going upward and onward instead of down and out, we need a renewed joint improvement program. Please give these questions and also your duties and responsibilities some thought over the

---

* H.P. Jacobi, *A Dentist's Flight Manual to Success,* Volume 1, DDS, Project P, Inc., 448 Edgewood Court, Neenah, Wisconsin.

weekend. We will discuss them over a cup of coffee at our next office conference.

1. What changes would you make for your benefit and the benefit of the patients? _____

_____

2. How would you change the current duties and responsibilities for yourself and the other personnel? _____

_____

3. What changes in the doctor's policies and attitudes, ideas and concepts would you like to see made? _____

_____

4. What other recommendations would you make if you were in complete charge? In other words, what would you change if it were your practice?

_____

Your staff may have the same inhibitions as your P/Cs. In fact, in addition to being your employees, they may also be your patients or clients. In this case, their opinions, suggestions, and criticisms will have *dual* importance. Yet these comments may never come forth unless they are requested.

Once again, be prepared for some surprises, both good and bad. The "feminine angle" is assuredly different and always worth noting.

And, as always, your concern and interest will be appreciated.

HOW TO DEVELOP PROFITABLE FEEDBACK
THROUGH "BRAINSTORMING"

The search for new ideas in a "thinking-up" session was discovered by Alex F. Osborn * of the world-famous Batten, Barton, Durstine, and Osborn Advertising Agency and is called "brainstorming." It is a system of group-ideation that is used today by government, business, education and the service professions to pool the creative talents of their members.

The basic principle of brainstorming is that no one person can have all the ideas but one person's ideas can spark a chain reaction. The basic problem is presented—whether it concerns products, people, or services—and a group of experienced people collectively use their ingenuity and their experience to find the solution.

Four Osborn ground rules give this technique its effective individuality. They are:

1) Criticism is ruled out. Adverse judgment of ideas must be withheld until later.
2) "Free-wheeling" is welcomed. The wilder the ideas, the better; it is easier to tame down than to think up.
3) Quantity is wanted. The greater the number of ideas the more likelihood of good ones.
4) Combination and improvement are sought. Suggestions by others on an idea give better ideas. Combinations of ideas lead to more and better ideas.

---

* Alex F. Osborn, *Applied Imagination,* (Charles Scribner's Sons, New York, 1963).

Here, for example, is just a sampling from fifty-one ideas produced by one brain-storming session on the subject of "New Services and Public Relations Ideas for the Modern Pharmacy." (The term "HH" refers to a "hitch-hike," a development of the preceding idea.):

1) Have a "Poison Antidote Information Service." Advertise this service in local media and through window display. Maintain a 24-hour-a-day answering service.

2) HH: Advise doctors, police department and fire department of this service.

3) Establish a "loaner" or "rental" service for wheel chairs or crutches used on a temporary basis.

4) Permit mothers to come in and weigh their babies on approved baby scales in the pharmacy.

5) HH: Give away a weight and date "scorecard."

6) The pharmacist who has an unlisted phone number should make it available to doctors in case of emergencies.

7) HH: Have this unlisted phone number with police and fire departments for emergencies.

8) Provide a special service for out-of-town college students. Give them a list of health products they should have with them, name of doctor, etc.

9) HH: Similar list of drug items for those who go on out-of-town or overseas vacations.

10) Scan the newspaper for announcements of engagements, weddings, business advancements, or recognition given to local customers. Send an appropriate note or occasion card.

11) HH: Cut out special items and have them plasticized as a permanent memento to send with a note of congratulations.

Does this list suggest any additional ideas (or "hitch-hike" ideas) that would be of value to a pharmacy or to your own practice? If so, the "ideation process" has begun.

Your staff can be a goldmine of practice-growth ideas, and brainstorming is an ideal way to go prospecting for profitable feedback.

A Kentucky practitioner treats his staff once a month to dinner and cocktails at a local restaurant of their choice. They use this out-of-office, social occasion as a brainstorming session to hash over any problems in the office, discuss new ideas for the practice and keep up to date with each other and their professional work. He has told me that he attributes the low turnover of personnel, the high espirit de corps, and much of the success of the practice to these enjoyable and productive get-togethers.

A Potlatch variation of this idea is the "ritual" established by a practitioner in Hawaii for any of his staff who have a birthday or "anniversary" with the office. On these occasions, they "celebrate" together with a two-hour lunch.

HOW TO OBTAIN INSTANT FEEDBACK

It was Robert Burns who wished that some power might "the giftie gie us to see ourand as others see us."

We have the gift. It is a tape recorder. Video and sound tapes permit us to see and hear ourselves as others see and hear us. Video tapes still require expensive equipment and elaborate setups. However audio tape recorders are an office byword and easy to use.

It has been estimated that each of us speaks an average of 30,000 words each day, enough to fill a small book. In the course of professional practice, the impact and effect of these words, regardless of their number, has double importance during P/C counseling.

Yet our seminar surveys show that very few practitioners have ever recorded their own voice during conversations with P/Cs—for the purpose of "feedback." (A playback from dictation or informal home recordings is different. It must be one's "P/C" voice.)

Those that have, invariably say their first reaction was one of "surprise," "shock," and usually "disappointment." The reason for this is because we hear our own voice from the "inside" while others hear it from the "outside." If you have never compared the two, you may not even recognize the sound of your recorded voice. It will be someone else's voice. Actually this becomes an advantage because it then makes it easier to be objective, to be critical if necessary, and to evaluate your reaction as a "P/C"—listening to yourself.

A tape recorder thus provides an easy way to monitor yourself and obtain instant and valuable feedback. Install one under your desk or in an inconspicuous place and record your next few conferences or case presentations. Take it home and listen through. You too, may be surprised.

YOUR TATTLE-TALE VOICE AND WHAT IT SAYS

Your manner of speaking, even more than your words, can "advertise" your personality, attitude and mood. Consciously or unconsciously, people react to your tone of voice, evaluate it, and give it their own interpretation—for better or for worse.

Studies of voice patterns at Stanford University show that it's possible to tell instantly whether someone's mood is good or bad, happy or out-of-sorts, by the way he answers even a simple question such as "How are you?" The standard answer, "Fine, thanks" won't tell you how he feels, but his voice pitch will reveal volumes. These studies show that when the response "Fine, thanks" comes over with a *rising inflection,* it means the person's in a good mood and *does* feel fine. Whereas *lowering* of the pitch is a dead giveaway that he does *not* feel fine, and tips you off that his answer is perfunctory and meaningless.

As obvious as these tonal inflections may be while *reading* them, and especially when *hearing* them, it's amazing how easily they are overlooked or forgotten while *speaking* to others. It happens because so much of the time we are more concerned with *what* we are saying than *how* we are saying it.

To keep themselves "on guard," many radio announcers will cup one ear, holding it forward so they can monitor themselves as they read. It enables them to "hear" themselves. (If you try cupping both ears, pushing them as far forward as possible as you read this sentence out loud, your voice will sound different than normally.)

To make you "voice oriented," here is a checklist of tattle-tale voice qualities and speech mannerisms that can creep into everyday, "off-guard" conversation, along with some possible P/C interpretations:

1) *Speech too fast.* This can occur if your instructions to the P/C are "routine material" that you have repeated hundreds of times before. To a P/C, hearing it for the first time, it can sound as though you are "hurrying through."

2) *Speech too slow.* Slowing down a little improves P/C comprehension, but slowing down too much can sound patronizing and belittling, as though talking to a child.

3) *Pauses that go unnoticed while speaking, but are painfully apparent on replay.* To a P/C, they may suggest "uncertainty" or "lack of confidence." This interpretation becomes more likely if speech is punctuated by frequent "uh . . . uh . . . uh . . . uhs." (One accountant admitted to me that he counted 32 of these unconscious "uhs" during his first recorded conference with a client.)

4) *Repeatedly clearing the throat* is a similar mannerism that many unknowingly have, yet is most noticeable to others. If it is *interpeted* as a sign of nervousness, timidity, or hesitation on your part, it will "shake the P/C's confidence" in your recommendations.

5) *Speaking in a monotone* is a very common fault of those who have never heard their own voices and aren't aware that it takes special effort to properly modulate. The P/C may mistakenly take it for "indifference" or even "boredom," which this colorless way of speaking suggests.

6) *Tonal variation* also affects the listener's reactions. You can call a 19-year-old boy Mr. *Jones* and make him feel important or call him *Mister* Jones and let him know you are making fun of him. Again, it's *how* you say, *what* you say that makes the difference. The right tone, at the wrong time can sound sarcastic, cold, or unecessarily formal.

7) *Voice is high-pitched.* Studies show that most people speak in too high a pitch, especially if they are under any stress or tension as for example when they are "rushed" or "trying to make a point" during a heated discussion. (The difference in "voice" between informal recordings and P/C discussions is usually one of "pitch.") To the unknown P/C, it has a tendency to sound "argumentative" or "high pressure." Combined with speech that is too fast, it may sound like "impatience" or even "anger." A low-pitched voice, on the other hand, is reassuring. It is more convincing and builds P/C confidence.

8) *Sloppy speech patterns,* dropped consonants, and slurred pronunciation certainly have an effect on "first impressions." To a stranger it may create "doubts" about your education and ability.

9) *Too many "technical terms."* Their effect on P/C comprehension and case

presentation has already been discussed in Chapter 9. Checking yourself on a tape recorder will reveal how often you (inadvertently) lapse into "technical language." Whether or not it sounds "pedantic" or "affected" will become more obvious while listening to the playback in your "P/C shoes."

Any or all of these unwanted and unintentional effects can be exaggerated by *non-verbal* communication such as raising an eyebrow, folding your arms and leaning back in the chair, looking away from the P/C or pointing a finger at the wrong psychological moment. That is why video-tape recording is currently being used in industry as the ultimate in self-monitoring.

Experiment with your voice by consciously changing the pitch. Talk fast, talk slow. Talk high, talk low. Compare the effects as a "P/C listener."

As a final check, imagine yourself as a "P/C," getting advice from the "person" you hear on the tape recorder. Do you consider his voice

pleasant?	down-to-earth?
sincere?	warm?
friendly?	assured?
interesting?	convincing?

In very practical terms: Would you buy a used car from this man?

Have fun monitoring yourself. Take yourself good naturedly. Don't try to alter your natural characteristics to the point where you appear unnatural. The very act of hearing yourself sets off automatic improvements by making you more conscious of your voice and the effect it has on others.

FEEDBACK—SPYGLASS ON SWITCHING

People are no longer awed as they once were by professional people. The mystique and "special status" are disappearing.

People are better educated, more skeptical, more suspicious, bolder, more outspoken, less patient, more demanding. Current writers have described the behind-the-scenes activities of many professions—the mistakes, the errors, the deficiencies.

As a result, P/Cs are "switching" from one practitioner to another a lot more readily if he fails to live up to their expectations, professionally or personally. Switching occurs in every practice. Some are leaving, some are coming all the time.

The purpose of feedback is to determine, when possible, why they are leaving your practice and why they have left another's. You don't want to repeat your mistakes and, if the mistake of another practitioner was personal rather than technical—as it usually is—you don't want to repeat it either.

Here is how to obtain feedback on "switching."

Screen your new P/Cs. Ask, "When did you last see a [comparable specialist]? What did he do for you?" Get the P/C talking about his previous experiences. The answers may be most revealing.

These questions cannot be construed as prying, since the past history is a vital part of the P/C's complete case history and, of course, might have an important bearing on the current status and/or future advice, treatment, etc.

If the "switch" was because of death or retirement of the former practitioner or because the P/C has moved from his community, the cause is obvious. If, however, the "switch" was the P/C's choice, you may well hear such complaints as:

> "He never explained anything."
> "He was always rushing and behind schedule"
> "He treated me like a child."
> "His attitude was very annoying."

Obviously, these comments are tip-offs to the P/C's sore spots, touchy areas and psychological needs. Let them be fair warning.

You might hear a complaint about "fees." This is worth exploring further, for if the former practitioner's fees and policies were reasonable, the "problem" will only arise again. In this case, *you* will be the one to lose the P/C *and* future good will.

If the former practitioner's policies were unreasonable or poorly communicated, if his fees were on a "take it or leave it" basis, without explanation, then your improved practice procedures will be most appealing to the P/C.

In order to effectively communicate to P/Cs, it is important to know something about their personality and psychological needs. This is not always easy in a busy practice. The "screening process" is useful as a shortcut to discovering these clues.

13

How to Keep Pace with Change for Continued Practice Growth

There is an old wheeze that says: Love is what makes the world go round. It isn't true. Love is what keeps it populated! *Change* is what really makes the world go round.

Change keeps us on our toes. It provides us with challenges in our jobs and in our daily activities. Every day our world undergoes a complete revolution, in living and shopping and eating and dressing and playing and learning and reading—and, of course, in our relationships with people, the basic component of every professional practice.

Professor John Goodlad of the University of Southern California said, "If the accumulation of knowledge is plotted on a time line beginning with the birth of Christ, it is estimated that the first doubling of the world's knowledge occurred in 1750; the second doubling occured in 1900; the third took only 50 years, to 1950; the fourth doubling of our world's knowledge then took only 10 years to 1960."

The fifth doubling of total information occurred in 1965, and knowledge is now expanding at the rate of more than 25 percent per year.

Our key problem, then, is not so much the initial education (that's a big enough problem), but the continued education of adults in the arts and sciences and the assimilation of an ever-growing flow of information.

CHANGE IS A CONTINUING SPUR TO SUCCESS

The key to practice growth and development is *change*—"keeping up to date." Those who don't keep up to date are, in a sense, behind.

One of the best means for practitioners to keep up to date and "on the go" is by reading the professional journals published in all professions. Monthly journal reading is a valuable investment in keeping abreast of the information explosion.

Another technique for keeping up to date is with pre-recorded tapes on subjects ranging from medical literature abstracts to foreign language studies and business skills. A number of commercial firms have made these available in cassette form, which can be played on portable tape recorders. I've met many practitioners who do this listening and learning while literally "on the go," such as driving to the office or on longer trips, when attending a meeting or convention.

The wide range of seminars for continuing education within the various professions is another important way of keeping pace with the demands of change. It is at these meetings—scheduled throughout the year either by universities, professional associations or private sponsors—that we are exposed to new ideas, procedures, techniques, and skills that enable us to better service today's P/Cs. They stimulate and accelerate practice improvement.

HOW TO STRETCH YOUR MEETING MILEAGE

Did you make a profit on the last seminar you attended? Was it just a trip to a distant city, a reunion with some colleagues and a banquet, or was it the beginning of a journey to improved practice procedures and professional success?

Seminar programs are serious business today and a costly investment. The dividends must be worth it. The world is turning faster and faster. Conditions are changing rapidly and we may not be able to apply yesterday's solutions to tomorrow's problems.

I have attended scores of seminars and workshops as a participant, but it is from the other side of the podium—as a speaker—that one discovers the secrets of getting real professional mileage out of them. Having conducted over 2,000 seminars for professional groups, and after "people-watching" nearly one-quarter of a million participants, I've seen firsthand the small difference in meeting-going techniques that can make a big difference in post-meeting results.

Here are some tested techniques for getting more mileage and results from seminars for the benefit of those attending them and in the interest of those who sponsor them.

1) Arrive rested, refreshed, and ready to go. To those who have worked twice as hard for days to carve out the necessary time, this may seem a tall order. But what a difference a night makes. If you can arrive in seminar city the evening before, condition yourself with a good night's sleep, eat a light breakfast, and walk around the block before the morning session. You can clear the cobwebs and be off to a flying start. Bring pencil and paper in case they are not provided.

2) Bring associates and assistants. Seminars are action programs. They often require changes in old habits, routines and attitudes. For these changes to be meaningful, effective, and started in your office without delay, your assistants and associates need to be "sold" on them.

If you go it alone, you may have to conduct the program over again when you return in order to overcome a natural enough resistance to change by a staff who possibly feels more comfortable doing it the old way.

You may be able to communicate the "information"; but, if you can't transfer the "motivation" as well, these innovations and improvements will come slowly, if at all. In the long run, it may be less costly and more effective to invest in their attendance at the program itself.

It's a psychological fact that an outside expert can often motivate more effectively than the practitioner himself who, although he's been saying the same thing all along, lacks the "authority" that is often attributed to public speakers. Illogical as it is, we are often impervious and indifferent to the sound advice of our closest associates and family. Yet an "outsider" saying the same thing becomes immediately convincing.

Furthermore, a staff feels complimented by inclusion in the trip and the subsequent decision-making process of change. Call it management by participation. It becomes a joint effort and the resultant team spirit and combined enthusiasm, we've been told, produces better results and more mileage.

3) Don't analyze the recipe, taste the cake. An audience can think faster than a speaker can talk. During the "time lag" there is a tendency to psychoanalyze the cook and then analyze his "recipe."

Consider the ideas and information more important than the speaker who is serving them up. The important man at the program is really *you.*

The next temptation, even more serious, is that many ideas may not make sense on paper or on first hearing. The recipe may sound impractical, full of flaws, if not downright impossible for *your* practice, *your* P/Cs, *your* area. Therein lies the danger. It may be discarded, without a test.

Remember the bumblebee? He weighs only 1.7 ounces; has a wing area of 2.3 inches which is at a dihedral angle of only six degrees. According to all the laws of aerodynamics, the bumblebee cannot fly.

But the bumblebee does not know this. Defying all theory, he flies merrily along.

As long as you have traveled this far (to the meeting), why not go one step further and test some of the ideas you've heard? The results may surprise you.

4) Seek improvement, not perfection. Be a prospector for nuggets, not for the whole gold mine. Don't wait for ready-made gems of wisdom. Be on your toes to recognize how a speaker's ideas can be modified, adapted and changed to make them valuable to your practice or P/C needs. Remember the old story of how little a pound of iron is worth and how much more valuable it becomes as it is changed into a pound of horseshoes, or a pound of needles, or a pound of watch springs?

5) Give as well as take. Don't be a deadpan at a seminar. Participate. Answer questions when they are asked. Ask a few yourself. Get involved. If a speaker should ask for a show of hands, go along with him. At my lectures, I continually pop "yes" and "no" questions at the audience; it's a ruse to get them into the act, to keep them alive, to rivet their attention. It creates spontaneity and frequently some repartee that makes the program more fun for everyone. It also tells the audience (as well as the speaker) how the participants feel about the subject under discussion and provides valuable feedback for all concerned.

The deadpan expression of an audience is the despair of public speakers. A single, appreciative face stands out and is a source of inspiration. It's an adage in show business that a responsive audience can turn an ordinary performance into an outstanding one. So *get* more out of your seminar speakers by *giving* more of *yourself.*

6) Have a system for taking notes—and using them. I wish I had a nickel for every idea that's been written down during a meeting by a well-meaning participant and later filed or forgotten. The antidote is simple:

List usable ideas as they come up. Keep them short so they will be legible and later will pop out at you. Then convert these to a numbered list, with the easiest to implement at the top of the list. Post it in a conspicuous place when you get back to the office as a "PLAN FOR ACTION."

Cross each item off as you complete it—one a day, one a week, one a month, but keep at it. In addition to better results, the "feeling of accomplishment" will be wonderful.

7) Meet and talk with colleagues. Talk with those who attend the program with you. Say "Hi!" to the speaker. Chat with the person on your right and on your left. Get together at coffee breaks and meals. Get involved in brainstorming sessions and kick ideas around. Profit from group dynamics and "feedback." See how others interpret and adapt. Bounce ideas off them.

8) Follow up energetically. Don't let the seminar die when you're through with it. Read books and articles that you hear about. Study the "take-home" literature.

Send "thank-you" notes to program chairmen, speakers, hosts, and exhibitors. Next time, you'll be greeted with open arms.

Follow up friendships. Keep in touch.

Keep your enthusiasm and interest alive as they supply the voltage for business success.

9) Adopt the positive approach. Don't concentrate on the reasons why a given idea won't work. If you win, you lose, because nothing gets done. Things remain "status quo." Devise ways to make ideas work.

Any idea for practice improvement is worth a try if it is ethical, dignified, and professional. The more "comfortable" you can feel with it, the more convincing it will be, but that will come with the time and practice.

Take any idea or practice procedure you're currently using that you know works. How "natural" and "comfortable" was it the *first time* you tried it? How "obvious" were its merits the first time you heard about it? Today, of course, it's become "second nature" and the "shortcomings," if any, have been overlooked and forgotten.

Try new ideas cautiously, conservatively, but think in terms of how they might be made to work. Try them for a few days. You'll discover quick enough if they're for you.

The positive attitude begets *change*; change begets *enthusiasm*; and enthusiasm begets *success!*

HOW TO CAPTURE THE ESSENCE OF NEW BOOKS

The printed word is the greatest source of knowledge. But the process that converts the printed word to practice procedure is an intricate one, with many trap doors to oblivion along the way.

—You can read it and not recognize its professional application in your practice.

—You can recognize the importance of what you read but then never think about it again.

—You can make notes for future reference but then never remember to refer to them.

—You can resolve to apply the new knowledge but never take the steps to implement it.

—You can take steps to implement the new knowledge but, at the moment of actual use, decide to stay with the tried and true.

Just as there are techniques to get more mileage out of seminars, there are techniques to capture the best of what new books offer your practice. Here are a few ideas I have gleaned from successful practitioners.

A book on a night table, for that few minutes of reading before you turn out the light, is more apt to be ready for that trap door to oblivion than is a book that is placed in a good spot for reading after you get up in the morning. Since practice-development ideas are stimulating, and since new technical developments require keen attention, early morning reading reaches a fresher and more receptive mind. An extra dividend from this is the ability to try out what you have read a few minutes later at the office. Interest and enthusiasm are not lost or dulled by intervening sleep.

Note-taking is valuable but can also be an exercise in futility. I have seen copious notes catalogued in a professional library and, by admission of the practitioner, hardly —if ever—referred to.

I believe in defacing a book. Write marginal notes, underline, fold back the tips of key pages, circle passages. I also believe it valuable to insert cards as markers and affix tabs that protrude from pages for instant reference. An old Chinese proverb says, "The strongest memory is weaker than the palest ink."

One practitioner had his assistant record on tape, key sections of practice management and technical books. The purpose was to provide a library of tapes, condensing important information from several books for the staff to utilize. An interesting by-product developed: After finishing the tapes, she would listen to the playbacks, often several times, to analyze her voice, diction and modulation. She took an interest in noting her progress from tape to tape; and as she absorbed the ideas they contained, she improved in an important facet of P/C relations.

THE GREATEST SOURCE OF ALL
FOR MEANINGFUL CHANGE

Seminars and books cannot teach creativity. Yet creativity is an important source of both technical and extra-technical practice improvements. In fact, personal creativity is perhaps the most important source for ways to humanize a practice.

Seminars and books do contribute, though, to an environment that is conducive to creativity. Good educators provide circumstances which develop creative behavior. When you leave a seminar or finish reading a book, you are likely to be in a more creative mood than when you started.

Creativity is first and foremost a willingness to break away from what is ordinary or expected. These are the greatest obstacles to creativity, and obstacles are *death* to creativity—they stop it. Remove the obstacles to creativity and it literally flows by itself.

Arthur Koestler has defined creativeness as the process of "bi-sociation," the basic ability to fuse two heretofore unconnected concepts or facts to form a single new idea.

The unfettered professional mind that is able to think horizontally and vertically is able to produce practice innovations and improvements to dwarf any he has heard or read.

Editorializing in a recent issue of *Psychology Today,* Nicholar H. Charney states: "No two snowflakes are alike, and yet all snowflakes are beautiful. Every human being is capable of great beauty, and life is a continuing kaleidoscope of human potential with man the creator." *

The successful professional is unaffected by uncertainty and negativity when it comes to change. He does not balk at changes because they are hard to make, risky or impractical. If he did, the chances are he'd *dismiss* change, not *adopt* change. Instead, he adopts the positive polarity, and views change as part of the creative process.

ENTHUSIASM MAKES THE DIFFERENCE

Dr. Norman Vincent Peale has pointed up the power of thinking positively and more recently has done an equivalently stirring job in showing how enthusiasm is the priceless quality that can transform careers, businesses and professions. In his *Enthusiasm Makes the Difference* ** Dr. Peale provides case history after case history of how small changes in environment and improvements in attitude can make drab days come alive and turn boredom into zest-packed living.

That is the message of Dr. Peale's book. It is also the message of this book.

But we have translated this message for use in the professional world—a world of

---

* Reprinted from *Psychology Today* Magazine, December 1968 (ⓒ Communications/Research/Machines/ Inc.).

** Dr. Norman Vincent Peale, *Enthusiasm Makes the Difference* (Prentice-Hall, Inc., Englewood Cliffs, N.J., 1967).

technically skilled practitioners striving to assist crisis-beset P/Cs, a world where this technical assistance is often aborted due to a communications gap.

We have held a mirror up to successful practitioners, that all may see the humanized dimension that exists in their practice—the Potlatch, the warm human concern, the skill at getting through to P/Cs the need for complete professional service.

This humanized dimension is the key to a successful practice. Many practitioners will see this and decide to make little changes in a humanized direction,

   changes in office decor,
   changes in routine,
   changes that add P/C comforts,
   changes in personal appearance,
   changes in case presentation,
   changes in attitude toward P/Cs,
   changes in manner of speaking,
   changes that add social amenities,
   changes that lead to better understanding,
   changes that create enthusiasm.

And "enthusiasm," said Ralph Waldo Emerson, "is the leaping lightning."

Enthusiasm, in action, resembles an upward wave:

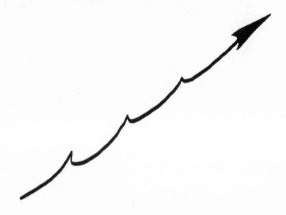

Something unusual happens to every little change. It not only affects P/Cs, it affects the practitioner. Self-actualization generates enthusiasm in the doer. We turn ourselves on by the very actions that are meant to improve life for the P/Cs. An oscillation is set up; this cycle reinforces the next, and so forth, until a crescendo of self-fulfillment is reached for the P/C and the practitioner alike.

An upward wave of professional success exudes, flows, radiates, attracts.

A Running Start

The dangers of a dehumanized society were recognized as far back as the nineteenth century and by such opposite minds as the conservative Disraeli and socialist Marx. Yet, today—with the increasing trends in professional practice toward group practice, delegation of responsibility to professional assistants, high-speed equipment, computerized procedures and third-party intervention—the depersonalization process is in high gear. Urgency is upon us.

That is why professional people who are the pacesetters in re-humanizing their practice are successful in every field. They begin at some point in their present practice; they make changes; and then things begin to happen.

If you are to join them, you too must make changes at some time in your practice. And that time is now!

If you put this book down and say, "Well, I'll try to remember the advice and see if I can stimulate enthusiasm and practice growth," I fear that your statement will soon be buried in the graveyard of good intentions.

To harness yourself to these ideas, to crystallize your thoughts into an active, dynamic program, write down your plan for immediate action.

Properly programmed, the mind can release those dynamic forces that can ignite practice growth, starting a chain reaction toward the accomplishment of your professional and personal goals.

FOUR STEPS TO IGNITE PRACTICE GROWTH— STARTING IMMEDIATELY

The explosive force is there. The fuse is set. Now you must ignite it. Here, from the success files, are four tested, proven steps that will get you off to a running start in the next five minutes.

Step One—
Write Down Your Long-Range Objectives

Review the Prologue. Make a list of professional and personal goals that are most meaningful to you.

Writing down objectives and goals has been found to be one of the best methods ever discovered for impressing goals on the mind and potentiating the desire to change. It becomes a personal commitment instead of vague, wishful thinking. It provides impetus and incentive and a "living" challenge that overcomes inertia and procrastination. It programs your mind for *action*.

Henry J. Kaiser, in a commencement address at the University of Nevada, drew upon his own life and experiences to offer sound adivce on "how to imagine your future." His number one recommendation was "know yourself and decide what you want most of all to make out of life. *Then write down your goals and plan to reach them.*"

"Practice growth" . . . "improved human relations" . . . "self improvement," these are, to be sure, goals. But, for the purpose of programming, they are vague.

Be specific.

How about: "I intend to double my present practice."

Think about it. Is it too challenging? To distant? Beyond your present reach?

Then break it down further. Segment your goal into bite-size pieces that are realistic, plausible, and easily attainable.

"I intend to add 2 percent growth to my practice every month."

This is an easy and a practical goal and yet it will double your practice within three years. It works this way:

100 (base for present practice)—with 2% added each month = *126.*

126—with 2% added each month for another year = *159,*

and

159—with 2% added each month for still another year = *200.*

You have doubled your practice at the end of the third year. Or, if you prefer, add only 1 percent a month and take six years. Now fill in your specific goals here:

Step Two—
   Visualize Your Plan

It whets the appetite and makes you hungry to achieve it. The appetite grows by what it is fed. It stimulates achievement-drive and multiplies it.

A few years ago, I met a California practitioner whose practice had reached the proverbial "plateau" in professional growth. His initial enthusiasm and momentum were waning with the passing years and being replaced by a negative polarity about almost everything. The symptoms were common enough.

One of our west coast seminars proved to be the "spark" that reversed this polarity. His antidote for negativity was interesting. The next day, he called an architect and proceeded to have plans drawn for a professional building that, until that point, had only been a dream. The plans were not for the entire building. He took easy steps. What he rendered was the exterior of the building, the facade, even the shrubbery—drawn to scale and in color.

His polarity, now reversed, caused things to happen. Nice things. Within two years, he had his building.

Another practitioner in Montana, caught in the doldrums of a practice that was just plodding along, got a swatch of bright orange carpeting from a local shop. He placed it in the corner of his private office as a symbol and a reminder of the plans he had made to redecorate and upgrade his office. His practice growth was ignited.

Recently, I received a letter from him that, in part, read:

> Finally got that private office built-on. Wood paneling with carpet, couch, lazy-boy chair, new colored metal desks and file cabinets. Really enjoy it. Reception room and business office have been repainted (yellow); new drapes and a wall-mural by a local artist. Also have added eight-track stereo tape player and music system.
>
> I have also started once-a-month staff meetings at the office; the object being to orient my employees towards practice growth and "potlatch" services.
>
> Since your seminar, a couple of pretty nice things have happened. First, I was appointed to the Montana State Board of Examiners and then elected Vice-President of the local Chamber of Commerce. Incidentally, my gross increased from approximately $35,000 a year ago to $50,000 last year, and we're shooting for $60,000 next year.

And it all started with a swatch of orange carpeting.

Still another way to visualize your plan and whet the appetite for "change" is to visit a practitioner whose success you would like to emulate. It's worth a cross-country trip if necessary. Spend a few hours observing him "in action" during a typical day. He'll be flattered by your request and the after-effects, I promise you, will put your enthusiasm in high gear.

Now, list your methods for visualizing your plans. The die will be cast.

Step Three—
Write Down the Means and Methods
by Which Goals Will Be Achieved

Itemize the specific activities and efforts that you feel will produce the desired results.

Take the marginal notes and starred items you've made in this book, while they are handy, and start your list. Begin with the simplest and least expensive measures. Add modifications and variations of these ideas. Cull out the ideas from other books you've read and the lectures you've attended. Get them in a workable order and add them to your list.

Put the major changes, additions and improvements at the bottom of the list. They'll be easier to tackle and incorporate, once the minor changes have proven themselves.

Note: Be sure to add a "re-investment" factor periodically throughout the list. It paves the way for practice improvement. Start with $50 a month, as though it were a fixed expense, and plan to spend it every month (or accumulate it for several months) for a major item. As it proves itself, increase the figure. Remember your practice is your best investment. Now write down your list of steps and methods.

Step Four—
Schedule a Timetable
for Completing This Program

Duplicate the tested success patterns established by industry and agencies such as NASA that have evolved from research to reality through a series of carefully planned stages and target dates.

Bracket a few items on your list and assign them a target date. Then set succeeding target dates by which you are determined to have the next group of items done. Spread the changes out over a period of time—a year or two. Refer to this timetable as you move along. It sustains the enthusiasm, the determination, the anticipation and, above all, the sense of accomplishment as each item is checked off.

This attitude of accomplishment is the very nourishment of success. Now write down your timetable for accomplishing the items listed in Step Three.

*You have set the wheels in motion
and have insured a bright, new tomorrow
in your professional life.*

Index

A

B

C